RIGHTSIZING
NATIONS

Also by
David Lockwood

Fooled by the Winners:
How Survivor Bias Deceives Us

Outplayed:
How Game Theory Is Used Against Us

Confused by the Odds:
How Probability Misleads Us

RIGHTSIZING
NATIONS

DAVID LOCKWOOD

RIVER GROVE
BOOKS

Published by River Grove Books
Austin, TX
www.rivergrovebooks.com

Distributed by River Grove Books

Design and composition by Greenleaf Book Group
Cover design by Greenleaf Book Group

Publisher's Cataloging-in-Publication data is available.

Print ISBN: 978-1-63299-633-6

eBook ISBN: 978-1-63299-634-3

First Edition

To my family

*Sometimes a peaceful divorce is better
than a painful forced union.*

—ALBERTO ALESINA and ENRICO SPOLAORE

CONTENTS

INTRODUCTION

For nations, size matters.

Larger nations can spend more on militaries. The United States can afford aircraft carriers; Costa Rica cannot. Larger nations can exploit economies of scale, spreading the costs of highways, schools, and police across a greater number of taxpayers. Larger nations can offer companies deeper markets to sell goods and services, unfettered by trade barriers.

But greater size comes at a price.

In a nation of one individual, the priorities of the government can be perfectly aligned with those of its citizens. Add another person, and disagreements may arise. The more people, the more potential for conflict.

As a result, a nation balances the advantages of greater size against the disadvantages of more disagreements among its citizens. The *optimal size* of a nation is one in which the advantages of greater size are worth the disadvantages of not getting exactly what any one individual wants. In other words, we are willing to put up with the inconvenience of a highway that does not run directly from our home to the office in return for splitting the construction costs with our fellow citizens.

Nations in which the benefits of greater size do not compensate for a greater divergence in priorities among citizens are *too big*. Nations in which the rewards of greater size would more than make up for a greater divergence in priorities are *too small*. These priorities include not only how taxpayer monies are spent but also the laws that dictate personal behavior, the rules and regulations governing commerce, and all the other ways in which governments impact the lives of their citizens.

Nations that are too small are unable to exploit economics of scale and are vulnerable to conquest by larger countries. Nations that are too big can suffer from poisoned politics and internal strife, as greater scale does not compensate for the divergence in priorities among citizens. If too small, nations are at risk from without. If too big, countries at risk from within.

Size often determines if a nation succeeds—or fails.

A nation can be rightsized through partition or annexation. But these measures have short-term costs paid for by those alive today, while the long-term benefits accrue to future generations. Political and economic elites may also fight any significant changes to the status quo, particularly when partitioning a country into smaller states.

A nation also can be rightsized by decentralizing the national government's authority or by transferring more authority to the national government. Decentralization pushes governance down to a regional or local level, rather than a one-size-fits-all national approach, and more closely matches the preferences of disparate populations within a country. But decentralization is much less effective than partition because a national government remains in place. Alternatively, a national authoritarian regime can enforce consensus through coercion. Consensus is a measure of the preferences of citizens, including the priority not to be punished or killed. A more powerful central government can employ both the "carrots" of a democracy and the "sticks" of an autocracy.

For a nation that is too small, increasing size may not be feasible, such as expanding the borders of a small island nation or a country ringed by high mountain ranges. Expanding the size of a nation through conquest has the high up-front costs of battle and the ongoing expenses of occupation that may not justify the advantages of greater scale.

For a nation that is too big, partition or decentralization may be unworkable because competing factions do not reside in separate regions within a country. Partition also risks civil war. If partition or decentralization is impractical, then the remaining option is to establish an authoritarian government to restore order and bind the nation together.

In this book, I discuss how to rightsize the United States and other nations. I explore the trade-offs between size and consensus, including partition, annexation, decentralization, and transitioning to a more authoritarian central government.[1] I start by defining the key terms of *states*, *consensus*, and *size* and setting out the theory behind the balance nations strike between the latter two items. I examine the five factors—incidence of warfare, cost of national defense, free trade, level of income inequality, and number of effective international government organizations—that primarily determine the optimal size of a nation for a given level of consensus. I then consider how these five factors have driven the formation of more than one hundred new nations during the last three-quarters of a century. I next weigh the costs and benefits of partition, annexation, and decentralization and analyze how the transition to a more authoritarian regime impacts the optimal size of a nation.

I hope to convince you that the five factors listed above have been shrinking the optimal size of countries throughout the world since World War II. I will also attempt to show that partition and decentralization are preferable to establishing an authoritarian regime for nations that are too big. And even if I can't persuade you of the advantages of partition and decentralization, I believe that after finishing this book, you will come away with stronger convictions of your own.

As we will see, nations that are too small have remained small due to geographical constraints or an unwillingness to annex other countries since World War II, with few exceptions. Over the same period, most of the nations that were once too big have partitioned. Hence, the explosion in the number of countries from seventy-four in 1945 to 196 in 2022.

But there remain a number of nations that are still too big and unable (or unwilling) to partition or decentralize. Unfortunately, for those nations, the remaining choices are to either continue to suffer from internal strife and political turmoil or transition to a more authoritarian regime. Some countries, such as China and Russia, have chosen the latter. Others, like the United States, are today struggling with the rise of autocratic populists who promise to bind the nation together by force.

We have decisions to make.

CHAPTER 1

STATES, CONSENSUS, AND SIZE

A *state* (or alternatively, nation or country) has been defined as "a politically organized body of people usually occupying a definite territory."[1] That definition, however, also fits other politically oriented groups, such as the Republican Party of Utah, the Policeman's Association of Kansas, or the Teamsters Union of North America. A state can also be defined as an organization that has been granted a monopoly on the use of violence, but this is not entirely accurate. Individuals sometimes commit acts of aggression, such as murder, against their fellow citizens without state approval.

A better way to define a state is to describe what it does: A state supplies public goods aided by coercion.

Public goods are distinguished from private goods in that they are non-excludable: An individual doesn't have to pay to get them. Public goods include a national defense, a police force, a legal system, a public education system, and environmental regulations. Many public goods are also non-rivalrous: You can consume them without reducing consumption by others. For example, national defense is non-excludable and non-rivalrous. A military force protects all, and an increase in population within a nation's borders does not require more soldiers. By contrast, public education is non-excludable but rivalrous. More students require more teachers.

The problem with public goods is that because a person doesn't have to pay to get them, there is an incentive not to pay. To ensure that everyone pays their fair share for public goods, states are granted the authority to use coercion, such as the threat of incarceration, to collect taxes, conscript armies, and enforce regulations. Coercion is necessary, because all citizens, regardless of their contribution to the state, receive the same public goods. With private goods, coercion is unnecessary, as a consumer receives a private good only upon payment.

Public goods also are generally one-size-fits-all. National defense, for example, is a public good that every resident of a country receives in a fixed amount, even though some individuals may prefer a stronger military, while others believe that the nation would be just fine with fewer tanks, missiles, and bullets. Environmental regulation is a public good that offers the same quality of air and water to all, regardless of the preferences of a country's residents. By contrast, private goods are customized to the specific needs of a consumer. There are hundreds of models of new automobiles that can be ordered with dozens of different options. Because of the one-size-fits-all nature of most public goods, individuals and companies are forced by the state to pay for public goods in amounts that do not match their preferences.

Consensus is defined as the average difference between the preferences of a state's citizens for public goods. Within a state, individuals surrender, voluntarily or not, part of their income in return for public goods. But individuals will demand different amounts and types of public goods. Some desire a single-payer government-funded health care system and others prefer a private insurance–based scheme. Individuals will also have divergent views on who pays for these public goods and how. Some support progressive duties on income, while others favor a flat tax.

Consensus is affected by more than the provision of what are traditionally thought of as public goods. States also impose a justice system with police and courts of law. States establish how commerce is conducted, such as the laws governing the exchange of goods and services, the transfer of property, and regulations concerning investment flows. Views on the above will differ among different segments of the population.

Because each citizen has a preference on the form and amount of public goods, we can expect consensus to be inversely correlated with population. A nation with a million individuals is likely to have a wider divergence of views on public goods than a nation with only a thousand. We also can expect less consensus in a more diverse country. Individuals self-identify along various dimensions, such as place of origin, language, or religion. The more individuals define themselves in ways that differ from others, the more likely that preferences for public goods will also diverge.

Hence, in this book, the *size* of the state is defined by population: the more citizens, the larger the size of a state. We could also measure size by geographical area. However, an increase or decrease in geographical size is not directly related to a corresponding change in the preferences of citizens, as fluctuations in land mass do not necessarily correspond with a gain or loss of consensus. The loss of an uninhabited portion of a country is not likely to impact consensus, and insurrections do not arise from lifeless regions. Instead, we measure size by population, because one of our underlying assumptions is that every individual is slightly different, and adding more people to a state will, on average, reduce consensus. For our purposes, Australia is a smaller nation than Malaysia, despite the former having a geographical footprint that is more than twenty times greater.[2]

THE OPTIMAL SIZE

Nations strive to strike the right balance between size and consensus. Greater scale reduces the cost per capita of public goods, so larger states can collect less in taxes or provide more government services. But as the population grows, the public goods supplied can become less closely matched to the preferences of many citizens. This mismatch can be offset with the benefit of lower taxes or more public services that greater size enables. Alternatively, the state could use the additional taxes from greater size to make transfer payments, in the form of money, goods, or services, to those portions of the population whose preferences diverge the most from the average citizen. In either case, states can offset an increase in size with measures to obtain a commensurate increase in the level of consensus.

These trade-offs help nations reach an optimal size. But there is not just a single optimal size for a given nation. In theory, a country that is at an optimal size could become larger or smaller and still maintain its optimal size. A country could elect to decrease its size and increase consensus, forgoing the benefits of greater scale in exchange for less internal strife. Or a country could increase its size and decrease consensus, gaining the advantages of greater size at the cost of more domestic turmoil.

Some countries that are too big cannot expand their territory to achieve an optimal size. If the United States conquered Mexico or Canada, the resulting nation would be even larger, as the decrease in the cost of public goods would not compensate for the fall in consensus from adding the populations of either of those countries. After World War II, Russia unsuccessfully tried this approach by annexing the Eastern Bloc nations of Europe.

By the same token, many nations that are too small can struggle to decrease or increase in size. Splitting a small island nation into several even smaller nations is unlikely to increase consensus enough to justify the increased cost of public goods. And due to geographical constraints, nations that are too small may be unable to expand. A nation that is made up of an island or group of islands surrounded by a vast body of water, such as the Philippines and Fiji, is constrained by the limits of population density from expanding in size. The same could be said for nations ringed by soaring mountain ranges, such as Switzerland and Bhutan.

THE FIVE FACTORS

In the Introduction, I outlined five factors that primarily determine the optimal size of a state:

1. Incidence of war

2. Cost of national defense

3. Free trade

4. Income inequality

5. International government organizations (IGOs)

Each of these five factors impacts the trade-offs between size and consensus in a nation as follows:

- The lower the incidence of war, the smaller the optimal size of a nation because less monies are required for military expenditures.

- The lower the cost of national defense, the smaller the optimal size of a nation for the same reasons as above.

- The more widespread free trade, the smaller the optimal size of a nation, since there is less advantage to the unfettered exchange of goods and services within a country.

- The greater the income inequality in a nation, the smaller the optimal size of that nation, because the greater the difference between the rich and poor regions, the greater the incentive for the wealthier regions to secede to avoid transfer payments.

- The greater the number of effective IGOs, such as the North Atlantic Treaty Organization and the World Trade Organization, the lower the incidence of war and the level of trade barriers and thus the smaller the optimal size of a nation.

Each of these five factors will affect the optimal size of a particular state in the same direction, but not necessarily with the same magnitude or yield the same level of consensus. For example, a lower incidence of warfare reduces the optimal size of all states. However, a particular country may have more warlike neighbors, which offsets the impact of a general decline in the incidence of warfare around the world. In addition, each of these five factors affects the optimal size of a nation *for a given initial level of consensus*. Nations have varying absolute levels of consensus—the residents of Singapore agree on a lot more than the citizens of Syria. The level of consensus between nations may remain widely disparate, even after the influence of these five factors.

If you are convinced that these five factors affect the optimal size of a nation as outlined above, then you may want to skip to Chapter 7. Otherwise, across the next five chapters, I will examine each of these factors in depth, starting with the incidence of war.

To illustrate how the incidence of war affects the optimal size of a nation, we'll start with a specific event in US history: the formation of the Department of the Navy in 1798.

This was the United States' second navy. The first had been abandoned.

CHAPTER 2

INCIDENCE OF WARFARE

THE FIRST (AND SECOND) US NAVY

In October 1775, the Continental Congress allocated funds to build the first American navy "for the protection and defense of the United Colonies."[1] But once the Revolutionary War ended and the new nation was at peace with Great Britain, the American government saw no reason to spend monies on a military force for the high seas, and the fleet was abandoned. For almost two decades after hostilities ended with Great Britain in 1783, the United States had no navy. That changed in 1798 with the founding of the Department of the Navy by President John Adams. By 1801, the US Navy boasted more than fifty ships.

The Department of the Navy was established to defend against both an old ally and an old foe. France was an old ally who played a critical role in turning the tide of battle against the British during the Revolutionary War. But after independence, French warships and privateers attacked American merchant vessels at will. By 1797, France and the United States had cut off diplomatic relations, and soon the two nations were in an undeclared war in the waters off the shores of the New World. At the same time, the United States feared an invasion by an old foe, the newly expansionist British. This fear turned out to be justified, as proven by the War of 1812.

The history of the first (and second) US Navy demonstrates how the demand for public goods can change. The US Congress was willing to fund a navy during the American Revolution and later when France attacked American merchant vessels and there were fears of a British invasion. But during the intervening years, when there was little or no perceived threat to the nation or American merchant vessels, there was no demand for national defense in the form of a navy.

This example of the funding and then defunding of the first US Navy illustrates that the demand for the public good of national defense depends on the incidence of warfare. As threats from hostile foreign powers increase, the size of the military necessary to defend the nation also increases. In a world of constant, all-out wars, only the largest nations with the size to fund the largest militaries would survive. In a world without conflict between nations, there would be no need for a military and greater size would not be an advantage. Between these two extremes, the demand for national defense is determined by the level of hostilities between nations; more peace means less ships, troops, and tanks. Therefore, *the lower the incidence of warfare, the smaller the optimal size of a nation.*

THE PUBLIC GOOD OF NATIONAL DEFENSE

Today, the provision of modern military forces is subject to significant economies of scale. A major portion of modern military expenditures are the up-front costs of training and research and development for large equipment, such as planes and ships. In addition, part of the military's job is to defend a nation's borders. The geographical area of a nation grows at the square of the radius, whereas the perimeter expands at a linear rate. Consequently, tax revenues will increase as a nation grows in size, assuming a constant population density, at a faster rate than the length of its borders. Hence, *a more populous state can fund defense forces at a lower cost per capita.*

While a larger military in theory enables a nation to conquer other nations, in practice, there are constraints on the size of a military that a state can sustain.[2] There has to be a sufficient number of nonmilitary workers to pay taxes to fund the construction and maintenance of military hardware and software, plus the salaries of those in uniform. A nation will collapse if there are not enough nonmilitary workers to produce consumer goods to sustain the population and fund the military. To survive, a nation must strike a balance between bread and bullets.

This balance was fundamentally altered by the Industrial Revolution.

THE INDUSTRIALIZATION OF WAR

The battlefields of the American Revolutionary War and Civil War would have been recognizable to the soldiers of both conflicts.

Not so for the killing fields of the twentieth century.

Before the Industrial Revolution, soldiers often supplied their own weapons, typically muskets, and before that, clubs, spears, and arrows. By contrast, modern militaries fight with manufactured fire-arms and machines supplied by the state. At the Battle of the Somme during World War I, Britain lost nearly twenty thousand men in a single day and millions died in the trenches of the Great War, slaughtered by mechanized weapons.[3] During the Battle of Verdun, approximately 200 artillery rounds were fired for every casualty.[4]

The weapons of the Industrial Age could also launch projectiles with greater destructive power. A bullet from a Civil War musket had the kinetic energy of 1,000 joules; a shell from a World War I artillery gun, 1 million joules; and a shell from a World War II heavy antiaircraft gun, 6 million joules.[5] A single World War II hand grenade contained TNT with the explosive power of 2 million joules.[6] One fire-bombing raid over Tokyo in 1945 released bombs with the equivalent of 60 trillion joules.[7]

The new technologies of the Industrial Revolution dramati-cally grew the ability to project power. Weapons of the Industrial Revolution were not only more powerful, but also had the ability to attack distant lands. Throughout history, a constraint on the size of military forces was the distance over which force could be pro-jected, which was primarily a function of transportation costs. For the first states, the reach of their military forces was severely limited. Legs determined the distance that could be traveled and shoulders the weight that could be carried.

For both ancient and modern warriors, the average weight a soldier can transport is about sixty pounds.[8] Vegetius, a Roman military official, wrote in the fourth century that "the young sol-diers must be given frequent practice in carrying loads of up to sixty pounds, and marching along at a military pace, for strenuous campaigns. They will be faced with the necessity of carrying their rations as well as their arms."[9] The British soldiers in World War I were burdened with an average of sixty-six pounds.[10] A typical soldier at the time carried about thirty pounds of nonfood items; the daily intake of solid food per soldier is about three pounds, so a soldier could lug at most about ten days of rations.[11] This meant that more than a week's march from the battlefield required lengthy and reliable supply lines.

Over time, as the cost of transportation fell, armies were able to extend their reach. A significant advantage for the North in the American Civil War was a vast railway network, thirty thousand miles in total—more than the combined track of the rest of the world—to transport food.[12] (It was also why a prime task of Union soldiers was to pull up Confederate track.)[13] Union quartermasters sent potatoes, vegetables, coffee, milk, and sugar over the Northern railroads to troops hundreds of miles away.[14] By contrast, the Confederate Army, without adequate supply lines, was frequently on the verge of starvation. As one Confederate soldier wrote his wife: "We have lived some days on raw, baked and roasted apples, sometimes on green corn, and sometimes nothing."[15]

With the advent of the Industrial Revolution, there was a dramatic drop in the cost of transportation. The machines of the modern world—engine-powered ships, planes, and missiles—enabled militaries to destroy an adversary halfway around the world. These machines could not only deliver on target projectiles at great distances, but also sustain the occupation of far-off countries. Driven by the ability to project power globally, the militaries of the Industrial Revolution were unparalleled in human history in terms of the ability to kill and to break things.

As a result, deaths from warfare dramatically increased during the nineteenth century, and that trend continued through World War I until the end of World War II. During the Middle Ages, less than 1 million people per century died from wars.[16] Estimated war deaths during the eighteenth century were 7 million.[17] That number rose to 19 million during the nineteenth century and then jumped to more than 110 million during the twentieth century.[18] Military and civilian deaths from World War II alone totaled more than 50 million.[19] The rising number of battle deaths (both soldiers and civilians) from the industrialization of war increased the demand for the public good of national defense from the beginning of the Industrial Revolution to the conclusion of World War II.

POST-WORLD WAR II: THE "LONG PEACE"

The risk of death from warfare took a dramatic drop after World War II. Because there has not been a global war in seventy-seven years, the latter half of the twentieth century and first two decades of the twenty-first have been called the "Long Peace." As one prominent author has written, "After 1945, the world's leaders said, 'Well, let's not do that again,' and began to downplay nationalism in favor of universal human rights, international laws, and transnational organizations. The result . . . has been seventy years of peace and prosperity in Europe and, increasingly, the rest of the world."[20]

The primary reason for the decline in battle deaths since 1945 has been an uneasy peace between the two great nuclear powers, the United States and Russia, which have protected their allies with a "nuclear umbrella." The threat of the use of nuclear weapons, also known as the doctrine of mutual assured destruction, seems to have worked as promised and stopped the outbreak of global war.[21]

As a result, battle deaths on a global basis have declined from more than two hundred to less than five per one hundred thousand people during the period from World War II to today.[22] Consistent with the Long Peace has been the sharp fall in spending by the most powerful military on earth. United States defense spending as a percentage of gross domestic product (GDP) fell from a high of 35 percent during World War II to 5 percent during the later stages of the Vietnam War and the Cold War and had dropped to 3 percent as of 2022.[23] The same holds true for other nations of the world as well, with global military expenditures, as a percentage of GDP, also steadily declining since 1945.[24]

Because of the sharp decline in the incidence of warfare since World War II, *a reduction in the demand for the public good of national defense has decreased the optimal size of nations.*

The incidence of war, however, is not the only impact on the optimal size of nations in terms of national defense. The cost to defend a nation is also a factor: if the military expense required to produce a given level of national defense is reduced, then a larger nation is less of an advantage.

I believe we are in the middle of a fundamental shift in the nature of warfare. This shift is dramatically cutting the cost of national defense, enabling peaceful smaller nations to effectively defend themselves against warlike larger countries for the first time in history.

CHAPTER 3

THE COST OF NATIONAL DEFENSE

The battlefield of the twenty-first century has become fundamentally different due to the advent of asymmetrical warfare, in which a nation with a vastly larger military force is unable to overwhelm a smaller foe without suffering devastating retaliatory strikes. Hence, *the lower the cost of maintaining a credible national defense, the smaller the optimal size of a nation.*

Atom bombs, bioweapons, and anti-satellite missiles are examples of weapons systems that characterize asymmetrical warfare.

ATOM BOMBS: MORE BANG FOR THE BUCK

Nuclear weapons are now within the reach of many nations and some non-state entities, due to technological advances that have lowered the cost of these explosives. Smaller countries are increasingly able to afford nuclear weapons, which can be used to carry out devastating attacks against the civilian populations of countries that are many times larger and more powerful.

One such small country is North Korea. The "hermit kingdom" has a population of 25 million and an estimated GDP of $18 billion.[1] About 1 in 100 people own a car. By comparison, the United States has a population of 328 million and a GDP of $21 trillion.[2] There are almost as many cars in the United States as people.[3] Yet the North Korean leader has summitted twice with former President Trump and with the leaders of Russia and China. North Korea has received billions in aid from other countries and serves as a disruptive force in the trade relations between the two great economic superpowers in the world—the United States and China. This for a country with a total economic output of less than half that of the state of Montana.

But North Korea has atomic bombs.

Other recent lessons of history may persuade smaller countries to develop a nuclear capability. Pakistan, another relatively poor small nation with nuclear weapons, receives billions of dollars a year in military and civilian assistance from the United States and others to help stabilize the country. And countries without nuclear weapons are met with threats rather than summits. The Iranian government agreed with the nations of the West not to develop nuclear weapons, only to have the United States subsequently withdraw from the agreement, cut all commercial ties, freeze Iran's assets overseas, threaten military action, and espouse regime change. The Libyan government surrendered its nuclear arms at the behest of the West, and the government was subsequently overthrown and the leader of the country, Muammar Gaddafi, executed. Evidence suggests that possessing nuclear weapons is a means to summit with world leaders, pocket billions of dollars in foreign aid, and secure a handy insurance policy against regime change.

With nuclear technology easier to purchase today compared to several decades ago, nations such as North Korea and Pakistan have been actively promoting their nuclear wares to other countries. Even China and India have sold nuclear technology that can be used to manufacture weapons-grade plutonium. For many nations today, developing atom bombs is simply a matter of the will to do so.

Two potential flashpoints in the world today illustrate the advantages of atomic weapons for countries confronted with larger conventional forces on their borders. Pakistan's army is a fraction of the size of India's, and most estimates indicate that India's military forces could overrun Pakistan in weeks. As a result, it has been the stated policy of Pakistan that an invasion by India with conventional forces will be met by a nuclear response. Israel is another country that would likely be overwhelmed by a conventional attack from a coalition of nearby countries. To prevent such an attack, Israel has promised retaliatory nuclear missile strikes launched from land, air, and sea, if provoked. In addition to land-based missiles in silos, Israel has fighters from the United States and diesel submarines supplied by Germany armed with nuclear weapons.

By offsetting these disparities in conventional military forces, atomic bombs serve as an example of the future of asymmetrical warfare, in which small nations can inflict massive destruction and loss of life on large countries. Unfortunately, once begun, nuclear proliferation will feed on itself. Many neighborhoods of the world today are nuclear-free, but they are not particularly safe places to live. If even just one nation arms itself with nuclear weapons, neighboring countries are likely to follow.

Recent history shows that possessing even a handful of nuclear weapons is sufficient to deter an invasion from other countries. Thus, as the costs of acquiring nuclear weapons—just like other advanced technologies—continue to fall, the advantages of size to fund national defense will also decline.

BIOWEAPONS: A POOR MAN'S ATOM BOMBS

Bioweapons contain tiny pathogens that are potentially lethal to humans. These stealthy armaments are dangerous because humans evolved to live in small bands of hunter-gatherers roaming across sparsely populated plains. By contrast, modern life is characterized by travel between densely populated cities on jet planes. By 2025, it is projected that 65 percent of the world's population will reside in cities with more than a hundred thousand people.[4] And given that every year 1.5 billion people travel by air,[5] a pathogen can be anywhere within forty-eight hours. Plus, humans are living longer. In 1900, 4 percent of the US population was sixty-five years old, and that demographic is expected to reach 25 percent by 2040.[6] But the elderly are more susceptible to viruses and bacteria. As the COVID-19 pandemic has shown, the world is at greater risk to pathogens than ever before. It is unlikely the COVID-19 virus would have spread through dispersed hunter-gatherer communities. We are more vulnerable to a bioweapon attack as the world becomes more urban, well-traveled, and older.

Bioweapons are cheap compared with other weapons of mass destruction. Epidemiologist Michael Osterholm has said that "an effective biological weapons program can be set up in a typical suburban basement, using basic high school or college lab equipment and materials easily ordered from a catalog."[7] And part of the appeal of bioweapons is that the origin of the attack can be difficult to pin down. A bioweapon can be deployed against an enemy by surreptitiously infecting a small group of individuals who then spread the disease to an entire population.

The *Textbook of Military Medicine*, the standard manual used for medical personnel in the US Army, states that "biotechnology itself may be the threat of the future, and not specific agents. . . . The employment of multiple chemical and biological agents is a very likely scenario."[8] One survey taken before the COVID-19 pandemic revealed that military strategists believed bioweapons posed a greater threat to humanity than nuclear arms.[9] Given the incubation period of many pathogens, the response of the defending country might be "too little, too late" to prevent an epidemic that kills millions or more. Of the fifty top bioweapons, only thirteen have vaccines or treatments.[10]

US health officials place bioweapons in three classes—A, B, and C—with A considered the most dangerous. The Class A pathogens are smallpox, anthrax, tularemia, plague, botulism, and viral hemorrhagic fevers. Each Class A pathogen has its own complexities as a weapon. For purposes of illustrating how a bioweapon could be unleashed, let's consider the first on the Class A list: smallpox.

Smallpox eradication is one of the great success stories of modern medicine. Unlike most other pathogens that can infect a range of different species, smallpox survives only in humans. When the World Health Organization announced in 1980 that smallpox had been eradicated in humans, it was a great day for medicine and humanity, as smallpox has killed more than an estimated five hundred million people throughout human history.[11] Once smallpox was eradicated, almost all countries stopped vaccinations. Because effectiveness of the smallpox vaccine declines after ten years, the number of individuals immune to the smallpox virus has been rapidly declining.[12]

Even though smallpox was eradicated, two stocks of the smallpox virus were retained, one at the Institute of Virus Preparations in Moscow and one at the Centers for Disease Control and Prevention (CDC) in Atlanta for research purposes. In addition, other countries with biological weapons programs are believed to have maintained stockpiles of the smallpox virus. Even if those strains of smallpox held by several governments were eliminated, the risk of a smallpox pandemic would not go away. In 2017, a Canadian researcher demonstrated that by employing the new techniques of synthetic biology, it was possible to recreate a version of the smallpox virus with $100,000 and genetic material purchased through the mail.[13]

A smallpox outbreak is challenging to contain because it is spread through airborne transmission, including air ducts in buildings, and has a ten- to fourteen-day incubation period.[14] This means that the disease can spread rapidly through a significant part of the population before health authorities are alerted that an epidemic is in progress. Launching a smallpox attack could be accomplished by spraying the virus from aerosol cans into confined spaces by attackers vaccinated against the disease. A silently infected person can infect ten to fifteen more individuals. The consequences would be devastating—smallpox is lethal in about a third of all untreated cases.

The emergency response to a smallpox outbreak is to contain the spread of the disease by an immediate inoculation program of the surrounding area, or "ring vaccination."[15] After the terrorist attacks of 9/11, the United States identified smallpox as a significant threat, and today the CDC has stockpiled enough smallpox vaccines for every person in the United States. However, the United States is unusual in that regard. Most countries rely on the thirty million doses of smallpox vaccine held by the World Health Organization in various locations around the world.[16] This means that most nations on the planet are vulnerable to a smallpox bioweapon.

The United States, while probably the country best equipped to respond, is still vulnerable to a smallpox attack. Smallpox vaccinations are risky for about 20 percent of the population whose immune systems are compromised by disease, steroids, medications, skin lesions, or pregnancy.[17] Additionally, smallpox vaccines are potentially dangerous for infants under one year of age.[18] Finally, a portion of the country's population is opposed to vaccinations of any kind imposed by civil authorities without consent, as we learned during the COVID-19 pandemic. To stop the spread of smallpox, a mandatory forced vaccination program would be necessary, even if such a program endangered the lives of certain segments of the population. Rounding up exposed individuals into quarantine centers and mandating travel restrictions for those in affected areas would also be needed. Confronted with civil resistance and outright evasion from a portion of the population, US health officials might be unable to establish a sufficient level of immunity through vaccinations to halt the spread of a smallpox outbreak. Even today, a substantial portion of the US population is resistant to taking COVID-19 vaccines and subsequent booster jabs.[19]

Regardless of the best-laid plans, the US health system—hospitals, doctors, nurses, labs, and so on—has not been tested by a biological weapons attack. In 2001, just before the 9/11 attacks, the United States practiced a mock smallpox outbreak, code-named

"Dark Winter," that started with a simulated release of smallpox in two shopping malls. Despite the best efforts of first responders and the US medical system, within two weeks the hypothetical epidemic had reached twenty-five states.[20]

In 2015, the Blue Ribbon Study Panel on Biodefense reported that "the United States is underprepared for biological threats. Nation states and unaffiliated terrorists . . . threaten us. . . . Biological events may be inevitable."[21]

We have advanced far beyond the hunter-gatherer communities that characterized the lives of humans for 99 percent of our time on Earth. But the features of twenty-first-century life that most of us enjoy—the amenities of densely populated towns, traveling easily and freely to all parts of the globe, and expecting to live to a ripe old age, aided by modern medicine—also make us vulnerable to biological weapons.

In 2013, genetic engineering experienced a major breakthrough with the introduction of Clustered Regularly Interspersed Short Palindromic Repeats, more commonly known as CRISPR. At a high level, CRISPR enables scientists to create synthetic RNA with which to "edit" DNA. The synthetic RNA targets a particular sequence of genes in the DNA of an organism and then replaces that sequence with a new one. In all subsequent replications, the altered DNA produces cells to match the new genetic instructions. More recently, researchers have applied artificial intelligence to CRISPR to improve the accuracy of the edits. The type of combinatorial task required of genetic editing, dependent on analyzing datasets with billions of vectors, is exactly the kind of work that supercomputers programmed with artificial intelligence are good at.

But there is another side to this developing technology to

reorder our genetic code. It is the dark side of genetic engineering, a field known as "black biology." The goal of black biology is to create even more deadly pathogens than those that exist today. In the years to come, the risks of a bioweapon attack will become even greater. Genetic engineering will enable state and non-state entities to create even deadlier pathogens than have existed in the past. That is because the declining costs and more widespread access to genetic engineering technologies that will advance medicine in the twenty-first century to new heights may also be utilized to construct the next generation of biological weapons.

In the past, scientists in biological warfare laboratories focused primarily on how to manufacture and deploy existing pathogens. In the future, using a combination of genetic engineering and artificial intelligence, those same scientists could be asked to make existing pathogens more lethal, or create entirely new pathogens that are vaccine- and antidote-resistant. The director of the Johns Hopkins Center for Civilian Biodefense has stated that "the quaint notion that you could list all the bad pathogens that might be made into weapons and just forbid them and scan the world for them is ridiculous. Because now all you have to do is click in the new gene, you get a new pathogen, you get a new weapon that isn't on the list."[22] The ability to alter an existing pathogen, or create an entirely new illness, presents a substantially greater risk to human populations than from any bioweapon in the past. The tools to reengineer how a pathogen infects and kills did not exist in the past. They are now in the hands of tens of thousands of scientists spread across nations throughout the world.[23] Governments that claim they are ready to defend against a biological attack may be only prepared to fight the last war.

Despite the ability to do so, no country is known to have attempted to deploy bioweapons on a global scale. In the past, the technology to launch a large-scale biological attack was reserved for the largest, most powerful nations on Earth. In the future, that technology may be deployed by smaller nations to defend or attack countries that are substantially larger.

As former Iranian President Akbar Hashemi Rafsanjani has stated, biological weapons are a "poor man's atom bombs."[24]

ANTI-SATELLITE MISSILES: MAD IN ORBIT

We are fortunate that nuclear weapons—at least not on a large scale—have not spread to space. Just like civilian populations, satellites can be held hostage to attack. Although for different reasons than Earth-based systems, the basic premise of mutual assured destruction (MAD) also applies to satellites in orbit.

The importance of satellites to military and commercial enterprises has dramatically increased in recent years. The armed forces of the world depend heavily on satellites for coordinating forces, missile targeting, and gathering intelligence. Satellite data is gathered to position not only ships on the ocean and planes in the air, but also individual soldiers on the ground. Satellites are also part of the lifeblood of a modern economy. The information supplied by GPS satellites is downloaded by every individual who owns a phone or drives a vehicle with a navigation system. Taking out an enemy's satellites not only blinds their military, but also cripples their economy.

While more than ten thousand satellites from more than forty countries have been launched, only about half are still in operation.[25] The rest are part of the ever-growing debris field in orbit around the Earth. The United States has launched over half of all satellites, including the global GPS system, operated by the US Air Force. It is estimated that 320 are active military satellites, of which the United States operates 173. Other countries with significant active military satellites include Russia (74) and China (68). Another sixteen nations are believed to have between one and ten each.[26]

Despite the critical role satellites play in defense and the economy, space remains to date a conflict-free zone, unlike the land and seas of the Earth. But the world's satellites remain unguarded and are therefore vulnerable to attack. The United States, Russia, China, India, Israel, and Japan are all thought to have some form of anti-satellite capabilities.[27]

In 1967, the United States and the Soviet Union signed the Outer Space Treaty, which banned nuclear weapons in space. At that time, the United States and the Soviet Union dominated satellite technology and accounted for almost all satellites in orbit. China and other major countries have subsequently ratified this treaty. One reason for such a treaty is that the cost of deploying weapons in space is estimated to be more than ten times that of deploying land-based systems.[28] Lifting heavy objects into space and then fixing or upgrading them once in orbit is prohibitively expensive. By avoiding a space race, nations saved themselves significant military expenditures. Another equally important reason is that space warfare is constrained by its own version of MAD, which fortunately does not involve people.

The US Space Surveillance Network within the Department of Defense tracks more than nineteen thousand orbital objects greater than two inches in diameter.[29] Given velocities of fifteen thousand to thirty thousand miles per hour, even the smallest bits of space debris can destroy a satellite. NASA was concerned that a paint chip that struck the space shuttle *Challenger* in 1983 upon reentry had compromised its structural integrity.[30] Tracking of these orbital objects is therefore critical, and satellites are regularly repositioned to dodge projectiles hurtling through space.

Half a century ago, the United States and the Soviet Union realized that taking out the enemy's satellites would quickly destroy virtually every satellite in orbit. In 2007, when China destroyed one satellite with a nonnuclear missile, it generated twenty-six hundred fragments that almost took down the International Space Station.[31] Destroying a sufficient number of satellites in space would make orbits around the Earth uninhabitable for all satellites because of a debilitating feature of space debris called "cascading."[32] A single collision of two pieces of space debris is believed on average to generate an additional five pieces.[33] The destruction of multiple satellites in orbit would set off a chain reaction of lethal projectiles circling the globe. This is space's version of MAD: The launch of an attack on enemy satellites is certain death for the satellites of the attacker.

Lethal space debris is also why satellites are vulnerable to asymmetrical warfare. A smaller rogue nation with anti-satellite missiles could destroy the world's satellites, crippling the economies and blinding the militaries of the largest nations in one swift blow. Of course, there could be immediate costs to the smaller country, including retaliatory strikes, but its economy is probably less dependent on satellites. And most smaller states possess no satellites at all.

After such an attack, the major nations of the world might attempt to clean up the resulting debris and relaunch new satellites. But so far, no technology has proven effective, despite numerous efforts, including nets and harpooning, at cleaning up space debris.

In the event of an attack on the world's satellites, a solution would have to invented and deployed. At any rate, unless the attacking rogue state was vanquished, it would not make sense to launch a cleanup, as another attack could just as easily destroy any new satellites put into orbit.

These factors have united the world's current leading military powers—the United States, Russia, and China—in efforts to discourage other countries from militarizing space and to comply with the 1967 Outer Space Treaty. But for a smaller, less economically developed nation, the threat of an attack on the world's satellites would be a strong deterrent to invasion by a larger, more powerful nation.

As we have seen, our world is in the midst of a fundamental change in the nature of warfare. The battles of the twenty-first century will increasingly be characterized by asymmetrical warfare due to the declining costs of deploying atomic weapons, bioweapons, and anti-satellite missiles. As a result, smaller nations will enjoy a reduction in the expense of maintaining a credible deterrent to even the world's most powerful militaries.[34] Therefore, *the declining costs of national defense have decreased the optimal size of nations.*

Similar to the cost of national defense, the level of free trade that occurs within the global economy also affects the optimal size of nations. To illustrate the impact of tariffs and other impediments to the exchange of goods and services across national borders, we turn to the Civil War era and the words of that vocal and outspoken critic of free trade: the sixteenth president of the United States, Abraham Lincoln.

CHAPTER 4

- - - - - - - - - - - - - - - -

FREE TRADE

"RUIN AMONG OUR PEOPLE"

In the years leading up to the American Civil War, the Northern states produced most of the nation's manufactured goods, while the economy of the Southern states largely depended on the growing of cotton, rice, and other commodities. During this period, US trade policy favored the North; high tariffs were placed on manufactured goods but not agricultural products.[1] As a result, prices for raw materials from the South were depressed by competition from foreign suppliers, while prices for manufactured goods from the North were inflated by prohibitive tariffs. Additionally, the United Kingdom and other European nations slapped import duties on all US manufactured goods. Without the South, manufacturers in the North would lose what was effectively a lucrative domestic free-trade zone without the trade barriers imposed by European countries. This provided an economic incentive for the North to stop the South from seceding.

Lincoln favored protectionist trade policies to protect Northern manufacturers and jobs, and this issue was one of the pillars of his campaign for president. His narrow victory in the 1860 US presidential election in the critical swing states of Pennsylvania and New Jersey was partly due to his support of high tariffs on manufactured goods. In one of Lincoln's stump speeches, he proclaimed, "When we buy manufactured goods abroad, we get the goods, and the foreigner gets the money. When we buy manufactured goods at home, we get both the goods and the money."[2] Lincoln also warned that "abandonment of the protective policy of the American government will produce want and ruin among our people."[3]

This example of US trade policy during the mid-nineteenth century illustrates the advantages of size in a world with trade barriers. A larger country offers broader domestic markets in which to sell goods and services, without the impediments to international trade put in place by other nations. Conversely, in a world without impediments to international trade, nations of any size can export products to the entire world. Therefore, *the more widespread free trade, the smaller the optimal size of a nation.*

THE INDUSTRIALIZATION OF TRADE

For most of human history, trade was a small part of everyday life because of a lack of specialization and the high cost of transportation.

Prior to the Industrial Revolution, the basic economic unit was the family. Just about everyone was a peasant farmer, sowing and harvesting grains and raising and slaughtering domesticated animals. Consumers and producers were the same people, and the capital used for production was a plot of land with the family farm producing just about everything most humans consumed. Consequently, there was no meaningful specialization of labor or movement of goods.

During the nineteenth century in the Western world, the Industrial Revolution changed all that. Factory workers were not able to be self-sufficient and traded wages for food, clothing, and shelter. A factory worker bought goods that were manufactured halfway across the globe and transported by ship or rail to a nearby shop. The cost of transportation also was prohibitively expensive prior to the Industrial Revolution. The movement of goods relied on human and animal muscle until external and internal combustion engines cut transportation costs dramatically. Steam engines powered ships that plowed the oceans and inland waterways. Soon afterward, steam engines were placed on steel rails, carrying bulk goods on long trains to the interiors of continents. By the twentieth century, the Industrial Revolution had severed the geographical ties between consumption and production, as trucks began streaming down highways and cargo planes began ferrying goods though the skies. With consumers in one country and workers in another, international trade exploded.

Despite the increasing specialization of labor and sharp decline in the cost of transportation, the United States and the rest of the world experienced a decline in trade as a percentage of the global economy from 1850 to the start of World War II. During that period, most European nations concentrated on trading with their own colonies rather than exchanging goods with other nations. In addition, during the period between World Wars I and II, international trade fell as nations attempted to "beggar thy neighbor" with prohibitive tariffs to boost domestic employment during the Great Depression. The trade walls between nations were built ever higher during this time, topping out with the halting of much international commerce in the days before the outbreak of World War II.

However, after World War II, the United States led a series of trade negotiations among the nations of the free world to remove barriers to international trade, culminating in the General Agreement on Tariffs and Trade (GATT) in 1947. Since then, there have been eight rounds of tariff cuts in GATT, with several rounds resulting in substantial reductions in trade barriers. The Geneva (1947), Kennedy (1963), Tokyo (1973), and Uruguay (1986) rounds sliced tariffs by 26 percent, 37 percent, 33 percent, and 38 percent, respectively.[4] Not surprisingly, global trade has increased 50 percent faster than world economic growth since 1980.[5]

With the dramatic growth in international trade has come the belief that all nations benefit from the unfettered exchange of goods and services across national borders. The conventional wisdom held among most economists and Western political leaders is that free trade is best for nations, large and small.

I question that belief.

THE THEORY OF COMPARATIVE ADVANTAGE

Those who espouse the view that free trade benefits nations of all sizes base their beliefs on an economic theory known as comparative advantage.

The basic idea of comparative advantage is "do what you do best and trade for the rest." The proponents of comparative advantage argue that this principle proves that everyone gains from free trade, regardless of a nation's absolute cost of production, which is partly a function of the size of a country. In other words, even if a country's goods and services are uncompetitive in international markets, it still benefits that nation to trade with others without restrictions.

This seems counterintuitive. Suppose a nation's cost of production of goods and services, after transportation costs, exceeds that of all other nations. In a world of free trade, this nation's goods and services would be uncompetitive in domestic and foreign markets. Yet the proponents of comparative advantage maintain that such a country, despite an absolute cost disadvantage in both foreign and domestic markets, benefits from unrestricted free trade.

To illustrate the argument made by the proponents of free trade, let's consider an example of a nation that has only two workers: a brain surgeon and a baker.

Suppose the brain surgeon is a really good baker, and the baker is not, at least compared to the brain surgeon. The brain surgeon can mix and bake a muffin in twenty minutes, but the baker takes two hours to perform the same task. This suggests that the brain surgeon should cook muffins for herself. After all, she is quicker at it than the baker. But the opportunity cost of time spent in the kitchen for the brain surgeon is high: The twenty minutes spent over a hot stove is time not spent manipulating surgical instruments over an operating table. Despite her absolute cost advantage in baking compared with the baker, the brain surgeon is better off purchasing muffins from the baker. If the brain surgeon baked her own muffins, her standard of living would fall, given the opportunity cost of time spent in cracking open eggs versus skulls. Of course, the baker, despite his lack of cooking skills, is better off if the brain surgeon buys muffins from him since the baker is not a brain surgeon.

By the logic of comparative advantage, even if the brain surgeon has an absolute cost advantage in brain surgery and baking, she is better off "doing what she does best and trading for the rest." Proponents of comparative advantage apply the same reasoning to nations. They argue that all nations are better off trading with one another, regardless of absolute cost advantages.

THE PROBLEM: UNREALISTIC ASSUMPTIONS

Comparative advantage is one of the most elegant theories that have been put forward in economics. However, in my opinion, it is based on unrealistic assumptions. That is why comparative advantage in the real world does not work as promised.

The first unrealistic assumption is that workers can easily transition between professions.

Let's expand our example to two nations, each with one brain surgeon and one baker. Suppose the brain surgeon and baker in Nation A are better at their respective trades than those in Nation B. In a world of free trade, Nation A would specialize in brain surgery and Nation B in baking, as everyone would have brain surgery in Nation A and consume baked goods from Nation B. But then the baker in Nation A would have to become a brain surgeon, and the brain surgeon in Nation B would have to become a baker. Maybe the former brain surgeon in Nation B will be OK with a lower-paying but less stressful occupation. However, the baker in Nation A would be unemployed, at least until he was able to graduate from medical school and complete a residency in brain surgery. The proponents of comparative advantage presume that a baker can easily become a brain surgeon. A critical flawed assumption behind comparative advantage is that the movement of labor between industries is immediate and frictionless.

In a world in which the baker in Nation A cannot gain entrance to medical school, Nation A would be better off with trade barriers. By putting up trade barriers on baked goods, Nation A ensures that the baker has a job. Of course, the brain surgeon and baker of Nation A will pay a higher price for baked goods, compared with a world of unfettered free trade with no tariffs on baked goods from Nation B. However, the declines in income due to the loss of the baker job and the costs of 50 percent unemployment in Nation A will likely exceed the gains from lower-priced muffins from Nation B.

In Western nations today, we can see the implications of this unrealistic assumption. Unskilled workers in the developing nations, led by China and India, have replaced unskilled workers in the United States and Europe. In effect, the bakers in Asia have replaced the bakers in the West. But the bakers in the West have not found new jobs as brain surgeons. In theory, bakers can instantly become brain surgeons. In practice, such a transition awaits a new generation of workers.

Free-trade advocates ignore the challenges of changing professions. In the United States, more than half of the 250 million adults of working age lack a college diploma.[6] Due to international competition, many have lost jobs and others have suffered a decline in income, as unemployment among unskilled workers has depressed wages. The average forty-year-old male high school graduate in America has a real hourly wage that is 8 percent lower than his father had in 1980.[7] Since 1985, the United States has lost an average of 372,000 manufacturing jobs each year.[8] As one commentator wrote, "The great winners have been the Asian poor and middle class; the great losers, the lower middle classes of the rich world."[9]

The loss of employment due to trade is a recent economic

phenomenon. Before the Industrial Revolution, everyone, other than infants and the elderly, had a job on the family farm, as there was more work than hours in the day. But an industrial or service-based economy does not guarantee a job for everyone. The only assurance is that prices and quantities will adjust to meet the supply and demand of the marketplace. That adjustment process applies to the price and quantity of the basic inputs of production: capital and labor.

Capital is simply delayed consumption. A person with $100 can choose to purchase $100 worth of goods now or hand over that money to another person in return for an agreement to give back the $100 plus an additional return, the price for delaying consumption. Individuals can decide whether to invest all or none of their money, depending on their preferences for current versus future consumption. The rate of return on investments therefore determines the quantity of capital in an economy.

On the other hand, price does not significantly affect the quantity of labor. If the price of labor falls below subsistence levels, the quantity of labor does not decline in the modern world. Starving to death enough workers so that the demand for labor matches the supply is neither politically nor morally acceptable. In fact, most nations provide support programs for the unemployed. Because price does not determine the quantity of labor, the supply of available labor can exceed demand.

Not surprisingly, industrialized economies throughout the world have suffered periodically from high unemployment. Pick almost any year in the last one hundred, since labor statistics have been collected, and there will be an industrialized country suffering double-digit unemployment rates. Even with heavy and forceful government intervention, the United States has experienced periods of high unemployment: 12 percent during the financial panics of the 1890s, 25 percent during the Great Depression of the 1930s, 10 percent during the 1973–1975 recession and first oil embargo, 11 percent during the Reagan recession of 1981–1982, 10 percent during the Great Recession of 2008–2010, and 14 percent during mid-2021 due to the COVID-19 pandemic.

And the number of workers out of a full-time job during these periods was actually significantly higher. The US government cleverly calculates the unemployment number to include only those looking for full-time work but cannot find it. But it is common during an economic downturn for some to give up looking for a job out of frustration or to take part-time work. During the Great Recession, the US unemployment rate topped 17 percent, adding back those who had given up looking for a job or had taken a part-time position.[10] This was 70 percent higher than the unemployment numbers reported at the time.

Free trade and the subsequent outsourcing of manufacturing to Asia has cost at least two million US factory workers their livelihood and much more.[11] Between 1999 and 2013, among white middle-aged adults lacking a college education, deaths from cirrhosis of the liver increased by 50 percent, suicides spiked by 78 percent, and drug overdoses increased by 323 percent.[12] As a result, from 2014 to 2017 life expectancy dropped in the United States for the first time in almost a century.[13]

The proponents of comparative advantage and free trade assume that displaced factory workers can easily and immediately find new professions. In theory, unskilled workers could transition to skilled labor. In practice, the transition from unskilled to skilled labor takes time and money. For many middle-aged and older workers, this transition will never occur.

The second unrealistic assumption is that global trade is characterized by perfect competition, in which no firm can influence the price or supply of a good or service. But many markets are dominated by a few large companies that leverage economies of scale to drive new entrants out of business, reducing competition.

In the past, some nations have implemented protectionist trade policies to scale up nascent industries to be able to compete in world markets. For example, the United States during the nineteenth century protected manufacturing with high tariffs. At that time, the United States had a comparative advantage in the production of agricultural products compared with the United Kingdom, whose companies had industrialized in the early nineteenth century, enjoying economies of scale that the nascent firms in the Americas could not match. If the United States had followed the logic of comparative advantage, allowing free trade with the United Kingdom, then the United States would have allocated its capital and labor to farm products, trading agricultural commodities for manufactured goods from the United Kingdom. Without trade barriers, the United States would have struggled for many years to achieve sufficient economies of scale in industrial manufacturing to compete successfully with the United Kingdom and other international markets. The advocates of comparative advantage and free trade at the time would have argued it was best for America to be a nation of farmers.

In the twentieth century, Asian nations similarly relied on protectionist trade policies to industrialize. China established special economic zones, funded state enterprises at below-market rates, and restricted imports.[14] South Korea and Taiwan subsidized large industrial firms and prevented foreign manufactured goods from entering the country.[15] All three countries manipulated their currencies.[16] These countries did eventually join the World Trade Organization (formed out of GATT), most notably China in 2001. However, they joined only after domestic firms reached sufficient economies of scale to compete in global markets. At that point, many Asian nations became proponents of free trade.[17]

As we have seen, following the dictates of comparative advantage and free trade can hinder a nation from industrializing. Proponents of comparative advantage argue that a country should specialize in products in which it has a comparative advantage. But that perspective fails to consider the implications for the economic future of a nation.

To illustrate this, let's return to our example of brain surgeons and bakers. Free trade between Nations A and B would yield the lowest prices today for the consumers in both countries. However, it could also result in relatively lower wages tomorrow for bakers in Nation B, as a nation of brain surgeons has a higher standard of living compared with a nation of bakers. The short-term gains of lower consumer prices would be far outweighed by the long-term losses in future income.

Policymakers in many countries, particularly in Asia, have been more forward thinking. They have realized that protecting infant industries through trade barriers, until economies of scale can be achieved, may have short-term costs but even greater long-term benefits. Protectionist policies initially force consumers to pay more for goods and services, but those short-term costs to consumers are often outweighed by the long-term benefits of higher wages for those consumers who are also workers. A country should consider the implications of free-trade policies not only on consumer prices today, but also on wages tomorrow.

A third unrealistic assumption is that exchange rates are determined by trade flows. Comparative advantage presumes that absolute cost disadvantages will be offset by a depreciating currency. The logic is that the more uncompetitive a nation's products are in price, the fewer will be bought, and the more products from other countries will be imported. This will reduce demand for the nation's currency, and the exchange rate will fall until that nation's goods are cost-competitive with foreign products.

However, exchange rates are driven primarily by investment flows. The average daily volume of foreign currency trades has been estimated at $3.2 trillion, while the average daily value of goods and services exchanged is $38 billion.[18] The United States is a prime example of the disconnect between trade and currency values. For decades, America has run trade deficits in the hundreds of billions of dollars. That should have driven the US dollar downward. However, investment flows into the United States have swamped the excess of imports over exports, and as a result, the US dollar has appreciated over time. In addition, exchange rates are also manipulated by governments. The People's Bank of China regularly intervenes in foreign exchange markets to achieve various political and economic agendas. Many other nations do the same. Because of investment flows and central bank interventions, exchange rates are frequently not closely tied to trade deficits or surpluses.

Despite these unrealistic assumptions, the theory of comparative advantage and the objective of eliminating all trade barriers are almost universally embraced by economists. The protectionist policy of the nineteenth century and the first half of the twentieth century in the United States, and in Asian nations in the second half of the twentieth century, has been condemned by most in the profession. A recent survey showed that 97 percent of economists believed that free trade was in the best interests of all nations.[19] Today, most economists see free trade as a "virtual ideology,"[20] with one famous economist calling comparative advantage "an intellectual *tour de force* of unusual brilliance" and the "deepest and most beautiful result in all of economics, an unassailable intellectual cornerstone."[21]

Reducing trade barriers is also part of the conventional wisdom among political elites. The exceptions seem to be some Asian leaders, who have built the fastest-growing economies on the planet. But most leaders of Western nations seem to believe that if a little international trade is good, then a lot is better. As long as this remains the conventional wisdom, unskilled workers in the United States and other Western developed nations will continue to suffer from lower wages or unemployment.

Despite the loss of income for many unskilled workers in the developed world, the barriers to international trade have been steadily declining since World War II. Hence, *the growth of free trade has reduced the optimal size of nations.*

There are clearly negative economic impacts on certain classes of workers from free trade, leading to greater income inequality. Next, we will analyze how income inequality impacts the optimal size of nations.

To illustrate, we will start by looking at the increasingly troubled relationship between one region of the United States and the rest of the nation. Some in this region are tired of sending billions of dollars more in taxes each year to the federal government than the value of the public goods they receive in return.

To rectify this imbalance, they propose secession.

CHAPTER 5

- - - - - - - - - - - - - - - -

INCOME INEQUALITY

GIVE AND TAKE

California is a "donor" state, receiving on average about 78 cents in benefits for every dollar paid to the US Treasury.[1] Compare this to Mississippi, a "recipient" state, which receives about three dollars for every dollar sent to the central government.[2] The disparity in these transfer payments, which add up to billions of dollars each year, is mainly because the average Californian is richer than the average Mississippian, although the greater value of a Republican vote compared with a Democratic vote in the Electoral College and Senate is also a contributing factor. This interstate welfare program is one of the drivers behind "Calexit," a movement whose followers advocate for the secession of the Golden State.

California is the fifth-largest economy in the world and certainly has the size to thrive as an independent nation. The state is more liberal than most other states, and if it were a sovereign nation, it might adopt different public policies, such as a single-payer health care system and more open immigration. A liberal California is part of the reason the United States is too big (see Chapter 10).

As a sovereign nation, California would have a higher level of consensus but a smaller size. From the perspective of many Californians, that's OK; it's better to pay more for what you want than less for what you don't. And it is not clear that Californians would pay more. The billions sent to other states through federal taxes would remain in California if it were a sovereign country.

California exemplifies the effect of income inequality on the optimal size of a nation. A richer region within a nation will favor lower transfer payments to a poorer region, while a poorer region will expect higher transfer payments as incomes in the richer region rise. Therefore, *the greater the level of income inequality, the smaller the optimal size of a nation.*

Redistribution of income from rich to poor regions would seem to be a strong incentive for wealthier areas to secede. But there are costs associated with secession, including the up-front expenses of separation such as a civil war. In addition, there are ongoing burdens from the loss of economies of scale in providing public goods. All of these costs need to be weighed against the benefits of eliminating transfer payments to poorer regions. On the other hand, poorer regions have a strong incentive for richer regions to stay. Poorer regions may discourage separation through threats of violence, while at the same time demonstrating some restraint in demands for transfer payments.

While a richer region may gain economically from secession, the nation as a whole will likely be worse off. The elimination of transfer payments does not change the average income of the country. Both the richer and poorer regions lose the economies of scale that characterize many public goods. Furthermore, a contested secession is costly in terms of lives and treasure, such as in the case of the American Civil War. The main benefit from secession is a higher level of consensus in the two new states post-partition.

INCOME INEQUALITY:
HISTORICALLY HIGH AND GOING HIGHER

Income inequality has been the norm during recent human history. Whether between rulers and ruled, or different classes of workers, there has been no period in which everybody was served equal slices of the economic pie.

The rulers of autocratic states over the last several thousand years rarely redistributed monies to their subjects. Prior to the Industrial Revolution, rulers and large landowners extracted almost all economic surpluses for themselves, while others toiled as subsistence peasant farmers. Agrarian economies were generally governed by some form of pharaoh, khan, emperor, king, queen, or other type of monarch, who colluded with large landowners to plunder most of the food supply beyond the minimum necessary to sustain the peasant population. Some inherited thrones. Others took them by force. It was only with the arrival of the Industrial Revolution and the shift of power to workers and capitalists that wealth became distributed less unevenly.

The Industrial Revolution permanently changed the economics of labor productivity and disparity of wealth, not only between the ruled and the rulers, but also among skilled and unskilled workers. Unskilled farmers left the countryside to become skilled workers in the cities, forming a large middle class, increasing the wages for many workers for the first time in human history. In turn, this newly empowered middle class replaced authoritarian rulers with political leaders more responsive to their needs, as the governors required the consent of the governed—workers and capitalists—to collect taxes. The fundamentally different nature of work in an industrial economy prevented the central authorities of modern states from extracting most of the economic surpluses for themselves.

As the Industrial Revolution progressed, machines replaced muscle, requiring fewer workers on the farms and leading to greater productivity. The first tractors could do the work of fifteen to twenty heavy horses, while today's modern tractors do the work of more than one hundred.[3] In addition, new crop varieties, higher fertilization rates, the invention of herbicides, and improved irrigation boosted crop yields.[4] These factors slashed the number of workers required to supply food to a nation. In 1850, farm workers comprised about 60 percent of the total workforce in the United States.[5] Today, that number has fallen to less than 2 percent.[6]

At the same time, skilled workers who could leverage their talents benefited more than others. In the early nineteenth century, physicians earned money based on the number of appointments multiplied by the price per appointment. Once no longer working, doctors lost all income. Today, a doctor might invent a new medical device that is used in millions of surgeries and retire early on the royalties. If a CEO successfully revamps the business strategy of a company with thousands of workers and billions of dollars in revenue, potentially hundreds of millions of dollars of incremental profits can be generated. That CEO can leverage her skills over a multinational company that sells to a global market. Other examples are the earnings of creative artists. Mozart played to a full house of kings, queens, and other assorted aristocrats, but the Beatles sold hundreds of millions of albums to adoring fans around the globe. Shakespeare did not starve, but J.K. Rowling has the income of a small country. In an industrial global economy, the productivity of a unit of labor varies widely by profession, because of the greater scale over which skills can be leveraged.

Taking advantage of economies of scale and global markets was an important part of the success of the Industrial Revolution. Without the additional efficiencies that size brought, the total economic pie would not have grown nearly as much. However, greater scale results in larger differences in labor productivity between workers, leading to greater income inequality. Hence, the disparity in incomes among workers is today greater than during the preindustrial period.

And there are no signs that this will reverse.

THE GREAT LEVELER AND AMERICAN GREATNESS

The United States is typical of the growing income inequality throughout the developed world.

The share of before-tax income of the top 1 percent of US households doubled after World War II.[7] Similarly, the average US worker's wages also doubled.[8] However, the progression of wage growth since 1950 has not been consistent. The period following World War II until the first oil shock of 1973 represented more than 90 percent of the wage gains for the average US worker.[9] The other 10 percent occurred after 1973.[10] Unfortunately, the average

US worker has not seen a meaningful increase in real income over the last five decades.

This rise in income inequality during a period of enormous wealth creation has brought populists to power in the United States, the United Kingdom, and other Western developed nations. A common theme among these elected officials is promising a return to the "better days" from the end of World War II to the early 1970s, when the average worker enjoyed real wage growth and income inequality was less extreme. In terms of the labor market for the average American and income equality, that period was a time of American greatness. Japan was still recovering from World War II. China, India, and Southeast Asia were under that thumb of communist regimes that smothered economic activity. For the workers of the West, there was little competition from foreign laborers.

By the 1980s, Japan had dug itself out of the rubble of World War II and fully recovered. During the 1990s, billions of workers in China, India, and Southeast Asia entered the global workforce, and this foreign competition depressed the wages of unskilled workers in the United States.

Another major source of income inequality over the last half century has been the gains the wealthy have enjoyed from global financial markets. These gains are in sharp contrast to the half century prior, in which the capital accounts of many of those at the top were wiped out by two world wars and the Great Depression, a period that has been labeled the "Great Leveler."[11] A dollar invested in the Dow Jones Industrial Average in 1929 was worth that same dollar in 1958, almost thirty years later. By contrast, a dollar invested in the Dow Jones thirty years ago, in 1992, is worth more than five dollars today. In 1980, yields on US government bonds peaked at more than 15 percent and then began a steady decline over the next forty years to less than 3 percent in 2022. That fall in interest rates lifted the values of stocks, bonds, and real assets, which are disproportionately held by the economic elite.

Populists may promise to make a country great again by returning to days gone by. But there are no signs that the workers of Europe and Asia will withdraw from global labor markets. Nor should we expect financial and property markets to retreat to the levels of the 1970s. A strong stock market has always benefited those at the top and, barring another Great Leveler, will continue to do so.[12] In addition, the reduction in trade barriers has forced workers of the developed world to compete with workers in the developing world, raising incomes of the latter at the expense of the former (see Chapter 4).

As a result, from 1950 to 2015, labor's share of US national income fell from close to 70 percent to less than 55 percent.[13] For more than a half century, the returns to capital have significantly outstripped the returns to labor.

THE ROLE OF PROGRESSIVE TAXATION AND PUBLIC SERVICES

During the nineteenth and early twentieth centuries, the primary job of the US government was the promotion of trade and the protection of person and property though the public goods of national defense and public safety. Beginning with the Great Depression in the 1930s, the main function of the US government, besides national defense, shifted to the redistribution of income from the wealthiest to the middle and lower classes. Progressive tax policies began to account for a rising share of taxes as a percentage of

GDP and today are the largest portion of the fiscal budget of most Western nations.

Before the twentieth century, the US government relied largely on tariffs as a source of revenues. It was not until 1913, with the passage of the Sixteenth Amendment, that a permanent income tax was imposed.[14] During World War II, Congress passed payroll taxes and exceptionally high marginal rates at the top end of the income scale, reaching 90 percent during the 1940s and 1950s. These high marginal rates were cut during the 1960s by President Kennedy and again during the 1980s by President Reagan to levels comparable to those today. Nevertheless, total US federal tax receipts as a percentage of GDP climbed steadily from less than 1 percent in 1900 to about 20 percent in 2021.[15] Most of the monies collected have been used to redistribute income, as Social Security and Medicare made up 60 percent of the fiscal year 2021 budget.[16]

Some have argued that Social Security and Medicare do not redistribute wealth but are just the return of payroll and other taxes collected in prior years. But current retirees receive three to eight times the amount they paid in taxes, including interest.[17] Going forward, the projected gap between what has been collected in taxes and what will be disbursed for Social Security and Medicare totals at least $21 trillion.[18] The burden to fund these programs does fall disproportionally on those with the highest incomes.[19] In 2018, the top 10 percent of income earners in the United States paid more than 70 percent of all income taxes, with the top 1 percent paying 37 percent of all income taxes.[20]

Hence, the steady rise in income inequality since World War II has been partially offset by the redistribution of wealth through taxation and supplying public goods to those who need them most.

FIRST MUSCLE, NEXT BRAINS

The United States and other developed economies are now in the midst of another economic revolution, in which machines are replacing brains. By the middle of the twenty-first century, machines programmed with artificial intelligence are expected to do the work of many unskilled workers and middle managers.

This trend will only accelerate over time, as machines have two distinct advantages over human brains: better packaging and more power.

Human brains are packaging-challenged. The human brain rests on top of a flimsy pedestal, the human body. If too heavy, the brain would cause us to periodically tip over, an evolutionary disadvantage when running away from toothy predators. As a result, natural selection has squeezed the brain into the small container of the skull. Furthermore, the brain has been optimized over millions of years to consume as little energy as possible, since food during most of human history has been scarce. Despite these evolutionary pressures, the human brain is still not energy efficient, comprising 2 to 3 percent of body mass while consuming 25 percent of total energy.[21] The total energy consumption of the human brain is about 20 watts.[22] By contrast, a modern supercomputer has no such physical constraints and does not need to be very energy efficient, fed by thousands of watts of power from the energy locked in hydrocarbons, streaming from the sun and radiating out of nuclear fission.

In addition to a superior package design and more power, machines evolve faster than humans. With each successive generation, engineers etch faster microchips and write more sophisticated programs. Machine evolution is also purposeful, driven by the goal to become ever more intelligent with each new version. On the other hand, humans evolve through random mutations of genes. Many generations may be born with no mutations for higher intelligence. The refresh cycle of the next generation of computers and cell phones is also a lot shorter than that of the next generation of children. And the basis for natural selection is that those with beneficial genes for survival produce more children. Evolution does not select for those who are more adept at linear algebra.[23]

Machine intelligence can also outpace human reasoning because electronic neural networks can be trained more rapidly for some tasks than any human can be taught. The human brain has a network of about 86 billion neurons, which are subtly tweaked as skills and knowledge are acquired. But the ability of human neural networks to learn is limited by the bandwidth of eyes and ears and relatively small amounts of memory storage. By contrast, a machine can input, output, store, and process vastly greater amounts of data. Human masters of the strategy game Go spend decades playing the game to gain the pattern recognition necessary to compete at the highest levels. AlphaZero, the program that defeated the world's best human player, trained its neural network in three days.

Today, machines can replicate in minutes skills that took humans years to acquire. In the future, the time required to train a neural network will continue to shrink, further narrowing the gulf between machine and human intelligence.

MORE MACHINES, FEWER WORKERS

In 2017, the McKinsey Global Institute (MGI) completed a study titled "Jobs Lost, Jobs Gained: Workforce Transitions in a Time of Automation."[24] MGI estimated that by 2030 at least four hundred million individuals could be displaced globally by artificial intelligence. While some people could be reabsorbed into the workplace as new jobs are created through economic growth, a majority would need to acquire new skills. The challenge is that the level of skills required for these new occupations is different than during previous economic transformations.

As the authors of the MGI study stated:

> *Unlike those earlier transitions, in which young people left farms and moved to cities for industrial jobs, the challenge, especially in advanced economies, will be to retrain midcareer workers . . . [so] workers have the skills and support needed to transition to new jobs . . . countries that fail to manage this transition could see rising unemployment and depressed wages.*[25]

MGI predicts that ultimately, between economic growth and new jobs created by the postindustrial revolution, the total number of jobs available will not decline. The question is whether the existing workforce can fill these new jobs, or whether it will require a new generation of workers with different skills.

Based on MGI's analysis, it is likely that the economy of the future will further skew income inequality. MGI warns that those not able to make the transition will be forced into low-wage, low-skill service work, such as caring for the elderly. MGI also concludes that this transition will be the most challenging in higher-income countries, such as the United States and Japan, and in Europe, as middle managers and unskilled workers are replaced by machines programmed with artificial intelligence.

In 2013, another major study was undertaken by the Oxford University Engineering Sciences Department, titled "The Future of Employment: How Susceptible Are Jobs to Computerisation?"[26] The Oxford study concluded that about half of all jobs in the United States could be partly or fully automated in the coming decades. After analyzing 702 occupations, the study found a wide disparity in jobs at risk. Workers most at risk are those in transportation, logistics, office, and administrative support, and those employed in routine labor on production lines.

The Oxford study describes the new technologies that will ripple through the economy:

> *First, as technology substitutes for labor, there is a destruction effect, requiring workers to reallocate their labor supply; and second, there is the capitalization effect, as more companies enter industries where productivity is relatively high, leading employment in those industries to expand.*[27]

In contrast to the MGI study, the authors of the Oxford study expressed skepticism that most workers will be able to make this transition: "From the perspective of the worker there is not much of a difference between work disappearing and being radically redefined. It's likely they'll lack the new skillsets required for the role and be out of a job anyway."[28]

The challenge for the workers of today is to retrain for the jobs of tomorrow. In the United States there are currently 3.5 million truck, bus, and taxi drivers.[29] Many are older and male, with a high school education.[30] But large portions of the US transportation infrastructure will eventually become automated. There are 3.5 million cashiers currently employed by US retailers.[31] At Walmart, the self-checkout line is almost always faster. Amazon one-click ordering is faster still. If today's workers cannot find new jobs, then unemployment will steadily rise until the next generation enters the job market.[32]

Thus, the challenges for the average worker today are only just beginning. When the Industrial Revolution replaced muscles with machines, humans were able to transition to knowledge-based jobs. However, once intelligent machines become better at most brain work, including reprogramming and maintaining themselves, there will be a lot less for humans to do. Humans are a combination of muscle and brain, physical and mental energy. There is no third category.

An analogy can be drawn to that of horses during the Industrial Revolution.[33] Although new machines—cars, trucks, trains—started taking their old jobs, horses were able to transition to new jobs that were less stressful, without the burden of lugging heavy carts. Horses have indeed found work in many recreational activities, and their lives are better than ever before. But the number of horses fell from 26 million in 1915 to 3 million in 1960.[34] Horses lost out because they could not compete with cars, trucks, or trains. For a horse to compete with a machine, it would no longer be a horse.

Similarly, humans eventually will not be able to compete with intelligent machines for some or parts of their old jobs. For a human to compete with a machine, it would no longer be human. Once intelligent machines are better at most brain work, there will be less for humans to do.

Of course, the pace and speed of replacing man with machine will have fits and starts. We have a natural tendency to want to deal face-to-face with other flesh-and-blood humans. When the telephone was first introduced, for example, some believed it did not have much potential for widespread use.

As an article in *Scientific American* at the turn of the twentieth century stated:

> *The dignity of talking consists of having a listener, and it seems absurd to be addressing a piece of iron . . . in order to use it a person was required to briskly turn a crank and to scream into a crude mouthpiece. One could faintly hear the return message but only if the satanic screeching and groanings of static permitted.*[35]

In the early twenty-first century, artificial intelligence is still at the "satanic screeching" stage and not widely used in many businesses. However, like the telephone, usage will improve over time, advancing on the goal set out in 1955 by Alan Turing that conversations with machines would become indistinguishable from conversations with humans. Recently, a "Turing test" was conducted between a machine and a thirteen-year-old boy speaking English as a second language. Thirty percent of the judges believed the machine to be the boy.[36]

Over time, the machines programmed with artificial intelligence will create an economy that requires a lot less help from humans. If a conversation with a machine is indistinguishable from one with a human, then it is not clear what tasks there will be for a human to perform, other than building more and better machines. This will not be the first time machines have eliminated entire professions. There were approximately five hundred thousand laundresses in private households in the United States in 1910, the year Alva Fisher filed a patent for the first electric washing machine. Today, there are too few laundresses to measure as a separate occupation.[37]

In the years ahead, machines armed with artificial intelligence will further widen the wage gap between workers. Without aggressive wealth redistribution policies by governments, income inequality will likely continue to rise to levels unheard of since the start of the Industrial Revolution. Hence, *rising levels of income inequality have steadily shrunk the optimal size of nations.*

Similar to the impact of rising levels of income inequality, the effectiveness of international government organizations, such as NATO to limit conflicts between nations, has reduced the optimal size of nations. And some of these international government organizations have also been effective at enriching themselves.

CHAPTER 6

INTERNATIONAL GOVERNMENT ORGANIZATIONS

OIL FOR FOOD AND DOLLARS FOR SADDAM

The United Nations Oil-for-Food Program was established by the UN Security Council in 1996 to allow Iraq, cut off from global energy markets by trade sanctions after the First Gulf War, to sell enough oil to feed its people.[1] Through this program, Saddam Hussein, the ruler of Iraq, was able to siphon off $1.7 billion in kickbacks and another $10.9 billion by smuggling oil. A UN report released in 2005, after the program was finally shut down, admitted that Saddam was able to divert billions because of "wide-scale mismanagement and unethical conduct on the part of some UN employees."[2]

Of the forty-five hundred participating companies, nearly half paid kickbacks or bribes. In addition, hundreds of individuals personally benefited. Benon Sevan, the UN chief for the Oil-for-Food Program, was indicted for receiving millions of dollars in payoffs and fled the United States to the non-extradition nation of Cyprus. Kojo Annan, the son of the then-UN Secretary-General Kofi Annan, collected $400,000 from a company that was part of the scheme.

Saddam used these funds to prop up his authoritarian regime and support his overextended military. The ill-gotten billions enabled him to perpetuate his reign of terror over the people of Iraq and rain missiles down on his enemies in the region.

The UN is the most prominent international government organization (IGO) in the world, but there are hundreds operating across the globe today. Some are effective and others are not.

The impact of IGOs on the optimal size of states is indirect. To the extent that IGOs bring about a more peaceful world, the amount spent on armed forces should decline and thereby reduce the advantages of size for funding national defense. IGOs can also work to reduce barriers to international trade, further decreasing the optimal size of nations. Therefore, *the greater the number of effective international governmental organizations, the smaller the optimal size of a nation.*

Some IGOs have as a primary objective the prevention of wars between states. In my view, these institutions, with the exception of a few military alliances, have played a limited role in preventing armed conflicts. The underlying reason most IGOs are largely ineffective is that they have too many members with too many competing objectives. In short, many IGOs are too big.

Prime examples of this are the League of Nations and its

successor, the United Nations. Both IGOs were set up to prevent wars. However, there is no evidence that either has made a significant difference in reducing the number of soldiers and civilians killed from interstate conflicts. The defenders of these IGOs claim that without the League of Nations and UN, there would have been more wars.

To consider the merits of this counterfactual argument, let's look to the historical record.

THE LEAGUE OF NATIONS: SPARROWS SHOUTING

Headquartered in Geneva, Switzerland, the League of Nations was officially inaugurated on January 10, 1920, after the signing of the Treaty of Versailles that ended World War I. The league began with forty-two members, reaching a peak of fifty-eight nations in 1935, before countries began dropping out as the world slid into World War II. The league consisted of a general assembly of all member nations and a council of fourteen states with four permanent members: France, Italy, Japan, and the United Kingdom. While actively participating, the United States never joined, fearing that membership would draw the nation into war. Germany became a member in 1926 but withdrew in 1933, when Hitler came to power. The Soviet Union initially refused, and then later joined the league, only to be expelled after the invasion of Finland.

Without an armed force, the league relied on the militaries of member states to compel compliance with council mandates. But member states proved unwilling to commit to collective action, despite passing flowery resolutions feverishly demanding military intervention. As the Italian dictator Benito Mussolini said, the league was "all very well when sparrows shout, but no good at all when eagles fall out."[3] The league could not even stop invasions by council members, such as the taking of Manchuria by Japan in 1931 or the annexation of Ethiopia by Italy in 1936.

There is no evidence that during the twenty-six years of the league's existence the frequency or severity of bloodshed around the world fell. There is no evidence of a major conflict averted. The league clearly did not prevent the carnage of World War II. In fact, it did not even pretend to try. The league abandoned its headquarters in 1939 and did not return until after the war.

The league held its last assembly in Geneva on April 18, 1946. In his final speech marking the disbanding of this ineffective IGO, one of the league's founders, Lord Robert Cecil, concluded with the words "The League is dead, long live the United Nations!"[4]

THE UNITED NATIONS: ON ACCOUNT OF THE UNITED STATES

The founders of the United Nations, many of whom were involved in the creation of the League of Nations, believed that the new organization would be different.

Unlike the League, the permanent members of the UN Security Council included all major postwar military powers: the United States, the United Kingdom, France, China, and Russia. Also, the UN is not solely dependent on the military forces of member nations, as it has its own peacekeeping force of more than a hundred thousand troops.[5] Known for their blue helmets, these soldiers, police, and staff officers are mostly drawn from the armed forces of member states. While the UN does not technically have its own army, these peacekeeping troops are under UN command and execute UN Security Council mandates.

The UN has undertaken two large successful peacekeeping operations: Korea and Kuwait. After the invasion of South Korea by North Korean forces on June 25, 1950, the UN adopted Resolutions 82 and 83 recommending members come to the aid of South Korea.[6] These resolutions designated the United States as the executive agent for leading a unified command under the UN flag. While technically a UN military force, the Security Council exerted no authority over combat troops, largely consisting of US military personnel. When the Korean Armistice was signed on July 27, 1953, the UN General Assembly approved the agreement but left the United States in charge of military operations.

This delegation of authority continues to this day. As UN Secretary-General Boutros Boutros-Ghali wrote in 1994:

> *The Security Council did not establish the unified command as a subsidiary organ under its control, but merely recommended the creation of such a command, specifying that it be under the authority of the United States. Therefore, the dissolution of the unified command does not fall within the responsibility of any United Nations organ but is a matter within the competence of the Government of the United States.[7]*

This UN peacekeeping mission has played an important role in preventing another war on the Korean Peninsula for over half a century. But that is not due to the UN. While technically a UN peacekeeping force, the troops lining the 38th parallel remain effectively part of the US military.

Similarly, the UN peacekeeping force in Kuwait was US-led. On November 29, 1990, the UN Security Council passed Resolution 678, which authorized members to use force to push Iraq out of Kuwait. (China abstained in exchange for lifting US economic sanctions, and the Soviet Union voted in favor in return for a $1 billion payment from the Saudis.[8]) A coalition of forces forced the Iraqi army to withdraw, and Kuwait was liberated. Although the United Kingdom, Saudi Arabia, and Egypt committed some military personnel, US troops comprised most of the combat forces, and soldiers from other UN nations were effectively under US military command.

The two most successful large-scale UN peacekeeping operations were initiated, controlled, and in the case of Korea, are still run by the United States. This has led some to allege that the UN is mainly a vehicle to further US interests. In a sense they are right: whatever credit is due for the UN's two largest peacekeeping operations should go to the account of the United States.

In addition, the UN has been powerless to stop several regional wars and conflicts. Examples include the Israeli-Palestinian conflict, the Kashmir dispute, the Cambodian genocide, the Vietnam War, the Somali civil war, the Darfur conflict in Sudan, the Srebrenica massacre, the Sri Lankan civil war, and the ongoing fighting in Syria and Yemen. The UN couldn't stop the US invasion of Afghanistan and Iraq after 9/11, or more recently, reverse the Russian invasion of the sovereign state of Ukraine.

The UN has had some successes: dozens of smaller peacekeeping missions, food assistance to millions of people, election monitoring in dozens of countries, and programs for refugee and maternal health. On the other hand, the UN unsuccessfully tried to limit the spread of the COVID-19 virus from China to the rest of the world. One of the main goals of its subsidiary, the World Health Organization—funded with $8 billion each year from member nations, including almost a half billion dollars from the United States—is to prevent global pandemics.[9] It failed. As one report concluded, "Although it was alerted in late December 2019 that a new disease had appeared in the Chinese city of Wuhan, the WHO continued to repeat Beijing's assurances that there was nothing much to worry about."[10]

While the UN on balance has been a force for good in the world, it has been ineffective at stopping wars (or pandemics).

Some supporters of the UN admit that no IGO can control the military forces of its member nations, and sovereign countries will always act in their own best interests, no matter how many UN resolutions of strong condemnation are debated and voted on. After all, the UN is not a world government.

But those who believe in the effectiveness of the UN also argue that it has made meaningful contributions to world peace by halting the proliferation of weapons of mass destruction (WMD). Supporters of the UN point to the fact that there has not been a nuclear or biological war since the organization was founded and that the UN has been instrumental in the negotiation and ongoing monitoring of the Treaty on the Non-Proliferation of Nuclear Weapons (NPT) and the Biological Weapons Convention (BWC).

THE NON-PROLIFERATION TREATY: SIGNATURE NOT REQUIRED

First negotiated in 1968, the NPT currently has 191 nations as signatories. More countries are a party to the treaty than any other arms treaty in history. The treaty is monitored by the International Atomic Energy Agency, an organization within the UN.

The NPT's main provision stipulates that "the NPT non-nuclear-weapon states agree never to acquire nuclear weapons and the NPT nuclear-weapon states in exchange agree to share the benefits of peaceful nuclear technology and to pursue nuclear disarmament aimed at the ultimate elimination of their nuclear arsenals."[11]

The NPT permits five states to possess nuclear weapons: China, France, Russia, the United Kingdom, and the United States. Those states, however, are not the only members of the nuclear club. India, Israel, Pakistan, and North Korea also brandish nuclear weapons, and those countries are not signatories to the NPT.

The NPT and the UN have been credited with the voluntary surrender of nuclear weapons programs in five countries. Over the last three decades, Ukraine, Belarus, Kazakhstan, Libya, and South Africa all resigned their memberships in the nuclear club. However, the NPT and the UN were not the main reasons.

In the 1990s, Ukraine possessed the world's third largest nuclear arsenal, stocked with more than five thousand strategic and tactical warheads. In 1994, Ukraine agreed to transfer its nuclear warheads to Russia. Similar deals were struck with the smaller nuclear arsenals of Belarus and Kazakhstan. The driving force for the surrender of nuclear weapons was Russia, who wanted those weapons out of the hands of its former satellites. In every case, the negotiations were strictly trilateral, between the United States, Russia, and each of the former Soviet satellite states. The existence of the NPT was not an important factor, and the UN did not play a significant role.

In 2003, Libya, an NPT member, voluntarily shuttered its nuclear weapons. The Libyan dictator, Muammar Gaddafi, had aggressively pursued atomic bombs from the time he first seized power. He unsuccessfully attempted to bribe officials in China, Russia, and India to sell him nuclear weapons. Gaddafi then resorted to black market purchases of nuclear materials but was unable to assemble a working device. However, under pressure, including threatened military action by the United States and several European nations, Gaddafi dismantled his nuclear program. In return, he received promises of aid and security guarantees from the West.

This turned out to be an unwise decision.

In 2011, a coalition of members of the North Atlantic Treaty Organization (NATO) invaded Libya and Gaddafi was killed by Libyan rebels. Libya was pressured by a group of NATO nations, led by the United States, to forgo its nuclear ambitions. The UN did not play a meaningful role.

South Africa's nuclear weapons program started with uranium mining in the 1950s and later licensing nuclear energy technology from the United States in the Atoms for Peace program. By the 1980s, the country had secretly assembled six atomic bombs with Israeli assistance. Government officials claimed later that the program was purely defensive, fueled by fears of an invasion by Cuban-backed Angolan forces. In 1988, South Africa and Angola agreed to a cease-fire, and fifty thousand Cuban troops were withdrawn. In 1991, the Iron Curtain fell, and Soviet ambitions to spread communism throughout Africa through proxies like Cuba evaporated. In addition, the South African government began planning in the early 1990s to hand over control of the government and military to the country's Black majority. South Africa formally announced the dismantling of its nuclear weapons program before relinquishing power to Nelson Mandela's African National Congress.

South Africa voluntarily surrendered its atomic bombs for a variety of reasons, particular to the circumstances at the time. There is no evidence that the UN or the NPT played a significant role in that decision. In fact, South Africa signed the NPT in 1991, two years before admitting that the African nation had built six nuclear weapons.

It is true that the number of nuclear warheads deployed by the United States and Russia has decreased dramatically from Cold War heights. Bilateral treaties between the two nations have eliminated more than thirty thousand nuclear weapons. But the UN was not responsible for those reductions either.

Overall, I believe that the NPT has not meaningfully reduced the proliferation of nuclear arms. Those nations that wanted nuclear weapons were either grandfathered into the NPT—or chose not to sign it. Those that didn't want them were happy to sign the NPT, and those nations that surrendered their nuclear arms did so for reasons unrelated to the NPT or UN.

This can hardly be considered a nonproliferation success.[12]

BIOLOGICAL WEAPONS CONVENTION: SIGN AND IGNORE

The Biological Weapons Convention (BWC) is a disarmament treaty, first signed in 1972 under the auspices of the UN, that bans the production and deployment of biological or toxin-based weapons. The BWC suffers from widespread and blatant noncompliance, as its signatories simply ignore their obligations. The worst offender has been Russia.

In 1953, after Stalin died, Nikita Khrushchev placed Yefim Smirnov, the chief of the Soviet Union's Red Army medical services during World War II, in charge of biological warfare. Smirnov, a medical doctor, led the Soviet biological program for the next twenty years, transforming what was a small intelligence operation into a strategic arm of the Soviet army. By the late 1950s, there were biological weapons facilities throughout the Soviet Union.

During the 1970s, despite signing and publicly avowing to abide by the BWC, the Soviets began dramatically expanding Russian biological weapons capabilities. By the late 1980s, the Soviet program, known as the Biopreparat, employed sixty thousand researchers and technicians with an annual budget of more than $1 billion. Biopreparat was tasked with developing and stockpiling pathogens, including new genetic hybrids of the most lethal diseases.[13] The Soviet program focused on altering existing pathogens to be resistant to treatment by antibiotics or immunosuppression, so that there could be no cure.[14]

In 1979, an accidental anthrax release that killed sixty-eight people in the area surrounding the Soviet biological laboratory at Sverdlovsk provided all the evidence needed to demonstrate that the Soviets were in violation of the BWC.[15] In 1989, Soviet microbiologist Vladimir Pasechnik provided firsthand testimony about Soviet biological weapons capability, and two years later, another Soviet scientist, known only by his code name, "Temple Fortune," gave similar testimony.

A major turning point came in 1992 when Ken Alibek, the deputy director of the Biopreparat, defected to the West. Alibek had extensive knowledge of the entire range of Soviet biological weapon programs and testified that the Soviets had mounted biological agents on a fleet of intercontinental ballistic missiles with sufficient smallpox pathogens to kill off any remaining Americans who might have survived a Soviet nuclear first strike. To support this program, the Soviets were producing twenty tons of fresh smallpox virus each year.[16] Missiles carrying anthrax were to be dispersed over New York, Los Angeles, Seattle, and Chicago. The Soviets believed that a single missile containing 100 kilograms of anthrax could kill three million individuals in a densely populated area.[17] Soviet scientists also developed a variant of plague that was more lethal than the Black Death that had killed a third of Europe during the fourteenth century.[18] They also genetically engineered a pathogen to create a deadlier version of Ebola.[19]

In response to these revelations, the United States confronted Russian President Boris Yeltsin with his country's violations of the BWC. Yeltsin claimed to be unaware of such programs and promised to promptly shut them down. In September 1992, Russia signed an agreement committing to convert the Biopreparat facilities to benevolent purposes. But the Russians have ignored this agreement, and in the years afterward have continued to research new bioweapons and stockpile old ones.[20] The current Russian ruler, Vladimir Putin, has approved an expanded biological warfare program called the Biological Shield of Russia.[21]

Verification is one of the challenges of enforcing biological warfare treaties. Unlike nuclear weapons, bioweapons can be developed and stockpiled in relatively small laboratories in ordinary-looking buildings throughout a country. Also, the equipment and staff for bioweapons have dual purposes, given that the tests conducted for the effectiveness of a vaccine are similar to those to determine the lethality of a disease. Personnel required for legitimate and not-so-legitimate biological research have similar educational and technical backgrounds.

Several other countries are also actively pursuing biological weapons with impunity. Iran, Syria, China, and North Korea are all believed to have biological weapons stockpiled, as well as ongoing research efforts to develop new pathogens.[22] These nations have been parties to the BWC for decades. Hence, there is no evidence the BWC, monitored and enforced by the UN, has limited efforts to develop and stockpile biological weapons.

THE UN: MOSTLY INEFFECTIVE AT MOST THINGS

In my view, the UN has been largely ineffective at stopping wars or the proliferation of atomic and biological weapons. One or more permanent members of the UN Security Council have vetoed 220 resolutions; Russia leads all nations in terms of vetoes with 112, followed by the United States with 81.[23] China has been the most agreeable, with only 11 vetoes.[24] A majority of UN member nations wish to abolish the veto power, but none of the permanent members are willing to consider this.[25] Due to disagreements between members, the number of resolutions that have passed each year has been steadily declining to just fifty-two in 2019—the lowest in six years.[26]

The UN's official website has a press release that includes the following words describing disagreements within the Security Council: "The Security Council remained largely paralyzed by expanding rifts and mounting tensions involving its permanent members . . . The Council's five permanent members remained gridlocked on several of the organ's oldest agenda items, with fresh divisions also emerging over newer issues."[27] As French President

Emmanuel Macron remarked in 2020, the UN "has such a hard time agreeing on so little."[28]

In short, the UN is too big.

On the other hand, there is evidence that some IGOs have made a difference. Some military alliances are composed of like-minded nations with a common goal. These IGOs have a size commensurate with the consensus of their member states.

The best example is NATO.

NATO: EFFECTIVE AT DETERRING RUSSIAN AGGRESSION

Founded in 1949, NATO is an IGO between the United States and many European nations with the primary purpose to prevent Russia from invading the NATO nations of Western Europe. To date, Russia has been unwilling to militarily confront a NATO country. In fact, one of the reasons Russia invaded Ukraine was the fear that the former satellite of the Soviet Union would someday join the Western alliance.

NATO is a collective defense pact: an attack on any NATO nation is considered an attack on all. By aggregating defense forces, NATO allows countries to economize on the public good of national defense. Excluding the United States, NATO nations spend, on average, less than 2 percent of their GDP on military forces. Fourteen countries, including several former satellites of the Soviet Union, have joined the alliance over the last three decades. The success of NATO is because the member states are united in a common goal: stopping Russian aggression against NATO members. NATO's thirty members share a common objective, in sharp contrast to the 193 members of United Nations who don't.

The United States subsidizes NATO by providing military forces and, at least in theory, covering the NATO countries with a nuclear umbrella. Because of this subsidy and stated willingness to risk the destruction of the United States homeland to save Europe, NATO nations have not lived up to treaty obligations to spend 2 percent of their GDP on military forces. As a result, former President Trump's administration made threatening noises about withdrawing from the military alliance.

But NATO has clearly served the interests of the United States. While supporting NATO, the United States has also been able to leverage military spending by European countries to deter Russian aggression. If forced to bear the burden of stopping a Russian invasion of every NATO country, the United States would have to significantly increase military spending.

Military alliances such as NATO are good examples of how, with the right balance between size and consensus, an IGO can reduce the incidence of warfare.[29] Thus NATO is an optimally sized IGO.

But IGOs can also work to promote more than peace.

THE WORLD TRADE ORGANIZATION: EFFECTIVE AT PROMOTING FREE TRADE

The IGO that has had the greatest effect on trade has been the World Trade Organization (WTO). The WTO and its predecessor, the General Agreement on Tariffs and Trade, have successfully torn down trade barriers around the globe. Studies have shown that without the WTO, trade between nations would have been significantly less.[30]

The 164 countries that are part of the WTO agree to grant

other members a most-favored nation status, subjecting each trading partner to terms no less favorable than any other nation. In effect, each WTO member receives the benefit of the most advantageous deal struck. To prevent cheating, WTO members agree to a dispute resolution mechanism that punishes offending nations with trade sanctions. One way to think about the WTO is like a club: if you violate the club rules, then you lose the privileges of club membership.

Of course, the WTO is not perfect. Tariffs are not the only form of protectionism. The United States and the European Union provide farmers with price supports. China subsidizes state-owned enterprises with loans at below-market rates. Nevertheless, the overall impact of the WTO has been to reduce barriers to international trade. Its members are united in a common goal that allows for the (relatively) free exchange of goods and services between nations.

Overall, the WTO is an optimally sized IGO.

The success of IGOs such as NATO and the WTO are due to an appropriate balance of size and consensus. There are other areas beyond defense and trade in which IGOs have attempted to play a role. The most notable is climate change.

Unfortunately, the priorities of the signatories to climate change agreements diverge significantly. This is particularly troubling because the implications of failing to address climate change threaten the continued existence of *Homo sapiens*.

KYOTO AND PARIS AGREEMENTS: COMING UP SHORT

In 1997, world leaders convened in Kyoto, Japan, and promised to reduce reliance on fossil fuels. At the time of the conference, fossil fuels supplied 80 percent of the world's energy demands.[31] Twenty years later, that number was 81 percent.[32] In 2016, world leaders met in Paris, France, and agreed to limit global average temperature rises to 2 degrees Celsius below preindustrial levels. The largest emitter of greenhouse gases, China, agreed to level off its emissions by 2030 but did not agree to limit emissions before then. India, another large emitter, agreed to limit its emissions but also not before 2030. The United States committed to cut its greenhouse gas emissions by a quarter below 2005 levels by 2025. In 2017, the US President announced that the country would pull out of the Paris Agreement, formally doing so in 2020—and then the United States rejoined in 2021 under a new administration. But climate agreements don't work on a four-year renewal cycle, and therefore the world awaits the outcome of the next US presidential election.

The Paris Agreement also carries no penalties because it was unpopular in many signatory nations. The cost of noncompliance is that some politician in the future will be accused of breaking a promise made by some politician from the past. With no meaningful penalty, the easy path is for politicians to promise now and let their successors apologize later. Despite plenty of summits and pledges by world leaders, not a single major country is currently on track to meet its pledges.[33] Few countries are implementing renewable policies to meet the commitments mandated by the Paris Agreement,[34] leaving progress on renewables 85 percent short of the agreement's goals.[35]

The Kyoto and Paris agreements are examples of IGOs that are too big and therefore largely ineffective.

THE ECONOMIC AND MONETARY UNION: EFFECTIVE FOR NOW

The Economic and Monetary Union (EMU) of the European Union is an agreement between European nations to a series of economic and monetary policies. The most significant of these has been adoption of the euro as a common currency by nineteen countries, known as the eurozone nations, that have surrendered control of monetary policy to the European Central Bank (ECB).

In my view, the EMU and its central bank, the ECB, together constitute the most powerful IGO in the world today—more important than even the UN. Outside the eurozone, no major developed nation in history has voluntarily ceded control of international trade and monetary policy to an independent supranational organization. The EMU determines international economic policy for most of the European Union, which represents 22 percent of global GDP, and the ECB determines the value of the euro, the second most important currency in the world.

The ECB was established as part of a political deal. In November 1989, German Chancellor Helmut Kohl was eager to reunify Germany after the collapse of the Soviet Union. But French President François Mitterrand, UK Prime Minister Margaret Thatcher, and other European leaders were concerned about the rise once again of the German nation. Mitterrand told others that a reunited Germany could "return [to] the world of 1913."[36] The president of France and the prime minister of the United Kingdom worried they "would find themselves in the situation of their predecessors in the 1930s who had failed to react in the face of constant pressing forward by the Germans."[37]

European leaders knew that Germany would never surrender political sovereignty to a supranational European parliament, but Mitterrand thought that Kohl could be convinced to give up some economic independence. A Germany that was more closely integrated with the rest of Europe, Mitterrand believed, would be less likely to cast (again) a yearning gaze toward his beloved Paris.

At a private meeting with Kohl in Strasbourg in December 1989, Mitterrand proposed a currency union of European nations, headed by an independent central bank.[38] Kohl knew that abandoning the Deutsche Mark and surrendering monetary policy to a central bank would be unpopular in Germany. However, Kohl felt he needed the support, particularly of France, for reunification and was deeply aware of the historical significance of the moment. As Kohl said later to a journalist, "Germany needed friends. . . . You are sitting opposite to the direct successor to Adolf Hitler."[39] The deal for a monetary union in return for unification has been described as "the whole of Deutschland for Kohl, half the Deutsche Mark for Mitterrand."[40]

It was an economic solution to a political problem.

Monetary unions have many benefits, such as reduced foreign exchange costs and often a more stable currency. However, the one-size-fits-all nature of monetary unions means national currencies can no longer appreciate or depreciate to absorb trade and investment imbalances between countries.

Germany has been the export powerhouse of the European Union based on its higher productivity of labor and greater capital investment. Before the euro was adopted, the Deutsche Mark steadily appreciated to offset trade surpluses from more competitive

German exports. However, with the introduction of the euro, the cost of German exports was now fixed in terms of the other European nations. By the early twenty-first century, Germany's trade surplus was more than $200 billion annually.

In theory, the other nations of Europe, in response to trade deficits within the currency union, should restructure their economies to compete with Germany by reducing labor costs and increasing investment. However, the prospect of French, Spanish, and Italian workers cutting wages and saving more to compete with Germans has not been politically popular. Rather than undertake these necessary structural reforms, other European nations have decided to issue government bonds to fund the trade deficits of the non-German nations. German banks, flush with the cash from trade surpluses, have been happy to lend the money.

Normally, a country that issues large amounts of debt to fund trade deficits will eventually lose access to the capital markets, as lenders doubt the ability of that nation to pay back the principal. This is particularly true given that none of the other European nations have been willing to do what is required to compete successfully with Germany.

But the political support for the EMU among European countries has given confidence to the debt markets that the ECB will ultimately bail out eurozone countries that get into trouble. Support of the ECB has allowed many countries to borrow at rates substantially lower than those justified by the ability of these nations to repay. For the governments of France, Italy, and Spain, it has been easier to issue government debt at submarket rates backed by the ECB than to ask voters to work harder and save more.

Some have suggested returning to the pre-euro days, allowing the Deutsche Mark to appreciate and the franc, peseta, and lira to depreciate, correcting the trade imbalances within Europe. This, however, is not in the short-term interest of Germany or the rest of Europe.

For Germany, the euro offers a currency that is perpetually undervalued. While Germany enjoys trade surpluses with the world, the rest of Europe suffers from trade deficits, which holds down the value of the euro. If Germany returned to the Deutsche Mark, currency appreciation would sharply increase the cost of German exports. At the same time, German banks are large lenders to other European nations. Abandoning the euro and restructuring European debt held by German banks would necessitate tens of billions in bailouts. For other European nations, the euro offers debt at below-market rates to fund domestic consumption, health care, and public pensions. Furthermore, quitting the euro would create substantial disruption to the broader European economy. One economist has written that "a collapse of the EMU would constitute the biggest economic shock of our age."[41]

Fortunately, there is currently a global glut of savings, so the ECB has been able to accommodate the steady rise in debt from the southern eurozone. Since 2008, the ECB has increased its lending, as measured by the balance sheet of the central bank, from 1.9 trillion to 8.2 trillion euros.[42]

The imbalances within the eurozone could be rectified if the southern European nations were willing to undertake the necessary reforms to compete with Germany. But none have been willing to do so. Consequently, the unemployment rate in Germany has remained persistently below that of France, Italy, and Spain. Breaking up the euro would allow changes in exchange rates to largely eliminate trade imbalances and force other European nations to take steps to restructure their economies to become more competitive. This is the right long-term answer—but the short-term costs would be high.

It is understandable why most Europeans support the euro. But I do not believe the euro is sustainable. Admittedly, it will take a debt crisis—similar to that suffered by Third World nations in the past—for Europeans to abandon the euro. At some point, once the ECB's balance sheet becomes overextended, the EMU will be confronted with the choice of abandoning the euro, at least for some southern European nations, or the ECB cranking up the printing presses and inflicting inflation on all eurozone countries. I doubt Germany will agree to the latter, given the nation's history.

Today, the EMU aided by the ECB is an optimally sized IGO. Its members, from the export powerhouse of Germany to the public welfare state of Greece, are united in their support of the status quo. Given a broad consensus among its member nations that quitting the euro would be just too painful, it should remain an optimal IGO—until the financial markets decide it is not. Like many sovereign debt crises in the past, investors will support the euro right up to the day they don't.

The trade-offs between size and consensus are no different for IGOs than for nations. Those IGOs that are optimally sized—NATO and WTO—are able to achieve their objectives. Those that are too big, such as the United Nations and the Paris Agreements, do not. The EMU is powerful today but may not be in the years ahead. In reducing the incidence of warfare and fostering the free flow of goods and services across borders, *effective IGOs like*

NATO, the WTO, and the EMU (for now) have decreased the optimal size of nations.

We next turn to the two ways a nation can alter its size. For nations that are too big, size can be reduced by partition. For nations that are too small, size can be increased through annexation.

But both partition and annexation have up-front and ongoing costs.

CHAPTER 7

PARTITION AND ANNEXATION

THE COSTS OF PARTITION

Breaking up a nation into two or more new sovereign states can be expensive. Equally problematic is that the costs of partition are paid up front by the current generation, while the benefits are realized by the generations that follow. A further issue is that political elites have a vested interest in a larger state; most national leaders have little incentive to surrender their current jobs. Economic elites may resist shrinking the size of available markets and the risk that trade barriers are subsequently erected between the new countries.

Partitioning a nation is more likely to occur when the transition costs are minimal. To overcome the intergenerational misalignment of interests and the resistance to disrupting the status quo, partition can be more easily justified if the long-term benefits substantially exceed the short-term transition costs.

In my view, two conditions must be met to avoid substantial transition costs when breaking up a country:

1. *Pre-partition functioning states.* The new states that are formed should have independent political and administrative structures in place before separating. Partitioning a failed state or creating a new failed state yields even less consensus and is likely to substantially raise the costs of separation.

2. *Limited migration post-partition.* The vast majority of the population should not feel compelled to move after partition. The citizens of the old and new states should have already largely presorted themselves and reside where they desire to live. Otherwise, the economic and social disruption of migration will dramatically increase the up-front and ongoing costs of partition.

Let's consider an example of the disastrous consequences when these two conditions are not met.

INDIA: DIVIDE AND EXIT

After World War II, the Labour Party that controlled the UK government decided to dismantle the British Empire. In 1946, the British prime minister dispatched a Cabinet Mission to India to arrange for a transition to independence by June 1948.[1] However, the Hindu-controlled National Congress and the Muslim League could not agree on partition. Meanwhile, ethnic clashes were growing increasingly violent. In August 1946, the Great Calcutta Killings left thousands dead and shocked the sensibilities of the British public.

In response, Lord Mountbatten was sent to India in March 1947 with the goal of ending British rule. Three months later, he announced that the British would relinquish control of India by the end of the summer. On August 14, the Muslim-majority Dominion of Pakistan was established (the modern-day equivalent of Pakistan and Bangladesh), and the next day the Hindu-majority Dominion of India was formed.

The abrupt partition of the country sparked the mass migration of fifteen million people. Hindus in Pakistan fled to India, and Muslims in India fled to Pakistan. In the chaos of this mass movement of religious groups, one to two million men, women, and children were killed in brutal ethnic cleansing, massacres, riots, abductions, and arson.[2]

The new states of India and Pakistan had not been established as functioning governments pre-partition. With the sudden departure of the British, the new states were unable to stop the widespread violence and destruction of property that resulted from the mass migration of millions from different ethnic and religious factions crossing the borders between India and the new nation of Pakistan. The two conditions for a successful separation—pre-partition functioning states and limited migration post-partition—were not met. As a result, the abrupt cleaving of British India resulted in a substantial loss of life and treasure.

By contrast, an example in which these two conditions were met demonstrates that separation can be achieved with minimal costs.

CZECHOSLOVAKIA: THE VELVET DIVORCE

Czechoslovakia was created in 1918 in the aftermath of World War I when representatives of the Slovaks and Czechs agreed to form a single nation. Part of the reasoning was that a larger country could support defense forces to protect the nation's sovereignty. But the country was still not of sufficient size to repel either the Germans or the Russians. During World War II, Hitler invaded and then separated Czechoslovakia into two countries, and Stalin then recombined the nations under Soviet occupation. With the collapse of the Soviet Union, Czechoslovakia became a democracy.

Czechs and Slovaks have been distinct ethnic groups for centuries, each with their own language, culture, and traditions. In addition, the Czech part of the country was wealthier and more industrialized. Before separation, there were large transfer payments each year from the Czechs to the Slovaks. And with the reduced threat of war from hostile nations, there was no reason to combine to fund a larger defense force.

After the collapse of the Soviet Union, the new democratic regime elected to lead Czechoslovakia forward could not hold the country together. Without the authoritarian Soviet regime, the two ethnic groups could not survive the transition to democracy. In 1992, the Federal Assembly of Czechoslovakia voted to split the country into the Czech Republic and Slovakia.[3]

The division of Czechoslovakia into the Czech Republic and Slovakia occurred without internal strife or loss of life because the two conditions for separation were met: pre-partition functioning states and limited migration post-partition. The new states of the Czech Republic and Slovakia had in place independent, stable, well-functioning political and administrative structures before separating. Czechoslovakia was already ethnically divided in two halves before splitting, so there were no large movements of people. This peaceful process of separation has been referred to as the "Velvet Divorce."

Since separating, Slovakia has enjoyed higher rates of economic growth than the Czech Republic by passing pro-business legislation and joining the monetary union of the eurozone. By contrast, the Czech Republic has become less business-friendly and maintains its own currency, the Czech koruna. Even today, most Czechs remain against adopting the euro.[4] In retrospect, each country had very different views on how to best manage its economic future. The Czech Republic and Slovakia split so the scale of each new state would equal consensus. As a result, both nations are now prospering, without significant conflicts between ethnic groups.

Under the right conditions, a successful partition of a country can be accomplished without substantial loss of life and treasure. However, in some cases, the short-term costs of breaking up a nation may be substantial and exceed the long-term benefits. Likewise, the current generation may be unwilling to bear the short-term costs of partition that benefit future generations. Grandchildren exert a strong pull on the heartstrings of grandparents; great-great-great-grandchildren, less so.

THE COSTS OF ANNEXATION

Like partition, annexation can be costly. In the past, the most common means to expand the size of a nation was through conquest. However, that can have substantial up-front costs, as war destroys lives and property in the attacking and defending nations.

Besides war, the unification of two nations has typically occurred through a wealthier country committing to transfer payments to entice a poorer nation to combine with it. Unlike partition, the cost of annexation is spread more evenly over current and future generations in the form of subsidies.

In my view, two conditions must be met to successfully annex another country without the high transition costs of war:

1. The annexed country must be willing to trade sovereignty for subsidies.

2. The benefits of greater economies of scale for the new nation must outweigh the costs of the subsidies to the annexed country.

There have been three annexations of significant size since World War II that met these two conditions, and so far, all three have been successful. In all three instances, the richer nation has offered substantial transfer payments to the poorer country.

NEWFOUNDLAND, ZANZIBAR, AND GERMANY

In 1949, Newfoundland voted to become the tenth province of Canada in a referendum in which Newfoundlanders voted for unification. As a much wealthier country, Canada has been able to provide substantial transfer payments to Newfoundland and connections to larger markets for Newfoundland's exports, primarily minerals, fossil fuels, and fish.

In 1963, Zanzibar ended its protectorate status with the United Kingdom and the next year merged with the mainland country of Tanganyika. The two nations were renamed the United Republic of Tanzania. Zanzibar is a poor country, whose main exports are spices, seaweed, and palms.[5] Much larger and relatively better off Tanzania has been subsidizing Zanzibar since unification with large amounts of economic assistance.

In 1990, East and West Germany reunited. At the time, East

Germany was significantly poorer than West Germany. By one estimate, West Germany has spent $2 trillion to rebuild the former communist country, almost bankrupting the reunited nation.[6] To this day, subsidies still flow to the former East Germany.[7]

For the richer nations, there were benefits to sacrificing some consensus to achieve greater scale. For the poorer nations, there were substantial subsidies to be gained.

We have seen from the above that countries have choices to decrease size through partition or increase size by annexation. But we also demonstrated in Chapter 1 that there is no one optimal size for a nation. There are trade-offs between size and consensus: A larger nation can partition into two or more optimally sized smaller countries just as a smaller nation can annex one or more territories to form an optimally sized larger nation. Given the many potential sizes of optimally sized nations, is it better to be a smaller or larger country? Does the size of a nation matter at all, as long as it is an optimal size?

SMALLER IS BETTER

Smaller countries are typically wealthier. Of the five most populous countries in the world, only the United States is considered rich. Of the twenty wealthiest nations in the world, only the United States is a large country. On average, economic growth is higher in small countries.[8]

Smaller countries in general are less violent. The Institute for Economics and Peace, a global think tank based in Australia, produces an annual Global Peace Index (GPI).[9] The GPI measures conflicts between nations as well as crime within countries on a scale from 1 to 5. A perfectly peaceful nation would have a score of 1 and the most violent imaginable a 5. Iceland tops the list as most peaceful with a GPI of 1.07, while Afghanistan lands at the bottom as the most violent, with a GPI of 3.6. Of the top twenty most peaceful nations, only Germany (16th) is a large country. The five largest countries are far down the list: China (104th), India (139th), the United States (121st), Brazil (126th), and Indonesia (49th).

Smaller countries tend to allow more personal and political freedom for their citizens.[10] Freedom House, a nonprofit organization based in Washington, DC, conducts an annual assessment of the political rights and civil liberties of the nations of the world.[11] The highest scores possible—that is, countries with the most freedom—are 40 for political rights and 60 for civil liberties. The sum of these two scores is called the Freedom Score. In the latest report, Finland, Norway, and Sweden tied for first with a score of 100. South Sudan and Syria scored a single point. Of the twenty freest nations today, only Japan (12th) is a large country.

Smaller countries often benefit from less political corruption.[12] Transparency International, a German research institute, has developed a Corruption Perceptions Index (CPI) that ranks countries from 1 to 100, from the most to the least politically corrupt, including the role of campaign contributions in elections.[13] In the 2021 survey, Denmark tied with Finland and New Zealand as the least politically corrupt country, and South Sudan ranked as the most corrupt. Among the top twenty least politically corrupt countries, the only large countries were Germany (10th), the United Kingdom (11th), and Japan (tied for 18th).[14]

Smaller countries overall have happier citizens.[15] Since 2012, the United Nations has published an annual World Happiness Report.[16] Individuals in member nations are asked a simple question: "Overall, how satisfied are you with your life these days?" The answer is given on a scale of 1 to 10, with higher numbers reflecting greater happiness. In the 2020 report, seventeen of the twenty happiest countries were smaller than average in population.[17] The report also shows that of the five most populous nations in the world—China, India, the United States, Brazil, and Indonesia—only the United States recorded an above-average happiness score.[18]

MORE CONSENSUS, ACCOUNTABILITY, AND COMPETITION

One reason that smaller nations are better places to live is that they tend to have a higher level of consensus. Of course, nations have varying levels of consensus. Some large nations, such as Japan, have a high degree of consensus, and some small nations, like Syria, do not. Regardless of absolute size, however, the larger the population, the more likely the priorities of a given citizen will differ from those of the average citizen. That's why we can expect smaller nations in general to suffer less internal strife and conflict and exhibit greater unity.

Smaller nations also benefit from less distance between the governed and the governors, at least in a democracy. In a small country, leaders can be held more accountable to their citizens. The same is true for government bureaucracies. And greater accountability aids in the fight against corruption.

In contrast to large countries, small nations have no choice but to compete in global markets, as domestic markets lack sufficient size to achieve economies of scale. Unlike large nations, small nations typically depend on international trade to obtain many goods and services—which means they cannot afford the luxury of trade barriers to protect domestic firms. This forces companies in small countries to be competitive not only at home but also abroad.

Small nations also have had to compete for citizens. China hasn't felt compelled to entice individuals to move there: the country has always had more people than it wanted. On the other hand, Singapore has had to offer some good reasons for people to relocate to a sandbar off the coast of Malaysia.

But while smaller countries are, on average, better places to live, there are costs, often substantial ones, to changing the size of a nation. For nations that are too big, the short-term costs of partition can outweigh the long-term benefits of a smaller state.

So, how do we explain the rise in the number of nations from seventy-four in 1945 to 196 in 2022?

CHAPTER 8

THE SHRINKING STATE

I n Chapters 2 to 6, I argued that five factors—the incidence of war, a reduction in the cost of national defense, reduced trade barriers, higher income inequality, and the establishment of several effective IGOs—have been steadily reducing the optimal size of nations since World War II. As a result, there has been increasing pressure for countries over the last seven decades to partition.

Those countries that choose partition can be divided into three broad categories. Of the new nations formed out of larger countries since the end of World War II, 70 percent were former colonies of mainly European powers, 16 percent emerged from the rubble of the former Soviet Union, and the remaining 14 percent were discrete examples of a larger nation breaking apart into two or more smaller countries. (See Appendix for a list of these nations.)

DECOLONIZATION

Of the 124 new nations formed since World War II, 87 were the product of decolonization. Colonization by European nations began in the fifteenth century and accelerated in the nineteenth century with the subjugation of parts of Africa, South America, and Asia, mostly by the United Kingdom and France and to a more limited extent by Belgium, the Netherlands, Portugal, Italy, and Germany. (After World War I, Germany's colonies were confiscated by the Treaty of Versailles. Their brief recapture during World War II and subsequent surrender is separate from the decolonization discussed here.)

Colonization was primarily driven by economics and national security.

Until the twentieth century, there were significant barriers to trade among nations. By establishing a colony, the home country could create a large free-trade zone without the impediments of tariffs and import controls imposed by rival nations. In addition, the home country typically sought to export manufactured goods to the colony and import raw materials, such as rubber, palm oil, nuts, or rice. For example, during the nineteenth century, India was the largest purchaser of British manufactured goods. In return, the United Kingdom was the largest importer of commodities from India, such as coffee and tea.

In most cases, trade between the home country and the colony initially raised incomes in both. Land was more plentiful than labor in the colonies, and the converse was true in the home country. The home country and colony could benefit from the former specializing in manufactured goods and the latter in agricultural products. However, given the lower wages in agriculture, this had the effect of increasing incomes in the home country more than those in the colony.

Furthermore, the home country typically set favorable terms of trade for themselves through forced bilateral agreements. Prices on manufactured goods relative to agricultural commodities were often established as artificially high levels relative to world markets. The home country also favored its own citizens over those native to the colonies. Land grants and mineral rights were frequently given exclusively to individuals and businesses from the home country, while natives were prohibited from owning or renting land or mines. As a result, natives were often relegated to laboring for foreign-owned companies at subsistence wages.

The home countries did provide some benefits to their subjugated subjects. Many Western nations constructed massive transportation networks, such as railroad tracks laid by the United Kingdom in India and canals and ports dug by France in Indochina. Of course, these expenditures were not purely altruistic. Transportation systems were vital to move commodities from the interior of the colonies to ships bound for the home country. These transportation systems also facilitated the movements of troops to defend against invasion by neighboring hostile colonies and other foreign powers.

Colonies were also important to national security as a source of military support for the home country. During World War I, 1.5 million soldiers from India fought in the trenches for England.[1] The French army included more than 150,000 troops from Upper Senegal and Niger and 160,000 from Algeria.[2] At the outset of World War II, more than a quarter of French infantrymen were from North Africa.[3] In 1940, a French general assured the country that millions of soldiers from French colonies could be brought to Paris to defend the capital against the Nazis.[4] The importance of colonial military support continued after World War II. In 1954, 59 percent of the French army consisted of conscripts from French colonies.[5]

However, the economic and political winds in the nineteenth century that swept European nations into a wave of colonization blew in the opposite direction after World War II.

The opening of world markets to trade in the 1950s and 1960s eliminated many of the advantages of a free-trade zone between home country and colony. For home countries, the benefits of purchasing raw materials on the global markets from whatever nation offered the lowest price outweighed the advantages of more favorable terms of trade with a colony.

At the same time, World War II had decimated the militaries and economies of European countries. Western European nations were now covered by the nuclear umbrella of the United States and the protection of a unified NATO. Therefore, the importance of maintaining large standing armies for the major colonial powers— the United Kingdom and France—diminished. Colonial soldiers were no match for nuclear weapons. European nations were also more reluctant to deploy military force overseas. The more liberal and war-weary democracies of the post–World War II era were increasingly reticent to send troops into the streets of their colonies to repress insurrection. Maintaining colonies required the will to brutally crack down on dissent.

After 1945, the United States and the Soviet Union stepped in to fill the political vacuum created by decolonization, actively competing for allies among Third World nations in the battle between capitalism and communism. Many colonies exploited this rivalry in return for substantial economic aid and security guarantees, as the security guarantees offered by their former European masters were now significantly less valuable. The United States was particularly forceful in twisting the arms of European nations to grant independence to colonies who would align against the Soviet Union.

With the dismantling of trade barriers and the decrease in the incidence of war, the optimal size of European colonial nations shrunk after World War II. Hence, the major European home nations became too big. This put pressure on the European colonial powers to partition.

For most, the cost of partition was minimal because decolonization did not result in failed states or mass migrations. Political and administrative structures had been established in the colonies to allow the home country to rule from a distance, and hence there were functioning governments in place pre-partition. The two populations—those of the home country and the colony—were typically separated by oceans and did not have substantial incentives to migrate. While elites from the home country lost position and power and some decided to repatriate, partition resulted in limited migration.

In most cases, colonization met the two criteria for partition without substantial up-front costs: pre-partition functioning states and limited migration post-partition. The long-term benefits of decolonization more than offset the short-term costs of partition.

THE COLLAPSE OF THE SOVIET UNION

After decolonization, the next largest source of new nations since World War II has been the freeing of the Eastern Bloc and other aligned countries when some twenty nations were formed out of the collapse of the Soviet Union.

After World War II, the Soviet Army chose not to withdraw from Eastern Europe, bringing many countries, including East Germany, Poland, Romania, Czechoslovakia, and Hungary, under Soviet control. Known collectively as the Eastern Bloc, these nations were police states, lacking open elections, a free press, or many of the personal liberties enjoyed by nations in the West. In East Germany, the Ministry for State Security, known as the "Stasi," enlisted one-third of the population as informants.[6] By occupying these nations after World War II, the Soviets were able to achieve the greatest expansion of the Russian state in the nation's history. By 1985 the population of the Eastern Bloc was 136 million, compared with the 272 million citizens of the Soviet Union.

But this was not to last.

The Soviet Union's expansion to include these European countries resulted in a nation that was too big. Not surprisingly, the Soviet occupation of the Eastern Bloc countries was punctuated by a series of uprisings. In 1953, a half million East German workers went on strike, shutting down the economy, and mobs burned government buildings. In response, the Soviets sent sixteen army divisions into East Germany, arresting more than twenty thousand people, and executing many others. In 1956, tens of thousands of Hungarian students staged protests, demanding free elections and independence from Soviet rule. Images of the toppling of statues of Stalin were printed in newspapers around the world. The Soviets sent more tanks into the streets of Budapest, and thousands of Hungarians were killed or imprisoned. In 1968, the Czech authorities in Prague began loosening state control over elections and the economy, an initiative known as the "Prague Spring." Fearing that other Eastern Bloc countries would follow, the Soviets marched troops from five other Warsaw Pact countries into Czechoslovakia. Hundreds of protestors were killed or seriously injured, and some Czech politicians were arrested and then imprisoned in the Soviet Union.

To curb rebellions, the Soviet Union subsidized the Eastern Bloc countries. The Soviet Union supplied raw materials and energy, such as oil and gas, to the Eastern Bloc countries in exchange for manufactured goods.[7] To discourage insurrection, prices for these commodities exported to the Eastern Bloc were set at below world market prices.[8] Manufactured goods from the Eastern Bloc, inferior to equivalent Western products, were also exported to the Soviet Union at artificially inflated prices.[9] This had the effect of raising living standards in the Eastern Bloc nations and depressing incomes in the Soviet Union. By the 1980s, the Soviet Union was estimated to be spending more than $20 billion annually in subsidizing trade with the Eastern Bloc—and that did not include substantial trade credits that were never repaid.[10]

The occupation of Eastern Europe after World War II did initially have national security benefits. These nations served as a buffer on the broad plain of Europe over which armies from Napoleon to the Nazis had marched to invade Russia. But the advent of nuclear weapons significantly reduced the value of the Eastern Bloc for national defense.

Furthermore, some in the Soviet military questioned the reliability of the Eastern Bloc armies. One Soviet general wrote:

> The significance of [Warsaw Pact allies] without nuclear rockets will be trivial. If somehow nuclear

*weapons are not used, then there are no guarantees
that say the Hungarians will unquestionably follow
the orders of our staff . . . they might even go over
to the side of the West. I strongly doubt the GDR
Germans will want to fight on Russia's side against
their western kinsmen.*[11]

By the 1980s, the costs of subsidizing the Eastern Bloc countries and maintaining sufficient troops to suppress opposition to
Soviet rule, added to the expense of funding a nuclear arms race
with the United States, had crippled the Soviet economy. In desper-
ation, Soviet leader Mikhail Gorbachev decided to institute a series
of reforms, including multiparty elections and liberalizing parts of
the Soviet and Eastern Bloc economies.

The liberalizations Gorbachev began in 1985 were the beginning of the end for Communist Party rule in Russia, culminating
in the 1991 election of Boris Yeltsin as president of Russia. Seventy-
three years of autocratic rule by the Soviet Communist Party was
over, and with it, the willingness to deploy military forces to keep
the Eastern Bloc nations under the thumb of Russia.

The fall of the Berlin Wall was followed by the overthrow of the
governments of the former Soviet Republics. Armenia, Azerbaijan,
Belarus, Bulgaria, Czechoslovakia, East Germany, Estonia, Georgia,
Hungary, Kazakhstan, Kyrgyzstan, Latvia, Lithuania, Moldova,
Poland, Romania, Tajikistan, Turkmenistan, Ukraine, and
Uzbekistan all emerged as sovereign states. With occupation of the
Eastern Bloc and other bordering nations, the Soviet Union had
become too big.

Like decolonization, the separation of the former Soviet

republics from the Soviet Union was achieved without substantial economic losses or widespread violence. There was limited migration post-partition because the citizens of the Eastern Bloc countries had no real desire to move to Russia. The political and administrative structures were already in place pre-partition in the former Soviet satellite states to carry out the basic functions of government and provide most public goods. The freeing of the Eastern Bloc nations met the two conditions for limiting the up-front costs of separation: pre-partition functioning states and limited migration post-partition.

While Russian leaders have since had second thoughts about partition, most citizens of the newly independent states of the former Soviet Union would agree that the long-term benefits of freedom from Russian rule were worth the short-term costs of separation.

OTHER EXAMPLES OF BREAKING UP NATIONS

Excluding decolonization and the collapse of the Soviet Union, seventeen new states have arisen out of ten existing larger nations since World War II. Rather than discuss each in more detail, let's look at some general observations about what can be learned from these partitions.

First, a low level of consensus by itself was not sufficient to push a country into partition. Rather, partition was more a result of excluding a significant portion of the population from representation in the state. If equitable power-sharing had been achieved, then there would have been a lot less motivation to secede. When one group dominates the government and excludes all others, there is greater risk of insurrection.

Second, civil wars occur mostly in poorer nations. There is a high negative correlation between income levels and the risk of civil wars.[12] For countries with a GDP per capita of $1,500 per year and above, the risk of civil war occurring during a five-year period is 3 percent.[13] Those odds increase to 6 percent for nations with a GDP per capita of $750 or less.[14] Poorer countries cannot afford other than a minimal level of public goods, so there is less motivation to remain part of a larger state. Poorer nations also have less monies to entice rebellious regions to stay and cannot afford a strong military to fight insurrection.

Third, civil wars frequently occur after a transition in government. Civil wars are five times more likely in the immediate years after a new nation is formed.[15] In the transition from being part of an empire or a satellite of a much larger country, states are prone to infighting as new power-sharing agreements are put in place for the first time.

Some have argued that there is a simpler explanation for civil war and the risk of secession: ethnic diversity. For some, ethnic diversity has been assumed as the best measure of consensus. In fact, studies have found correlations between the prevalence of civil war and ethnic diversity. Since 1945, thirty-nine of forty secession movements that have resulted in battle deaths of more than a thousand soldiers have been fought along ethnic lines.[16]

But I believe the apparent link between ethnic diversity and civil conflict is an instance of mistaking correlation for causation.

Secession movements typically do not become civil wars unless most of the individuals seeking to form a new country already reside in one place. Secession movements are sparked by polarization and exclusion, but a successful secession movement requires a place in which to secede. Ethnicity is related to civil war in that most groups do not attempt to secede unless they already reside in and dominate a particular region of a nation. For example, ethnic groups are more likely to start civil wars than high-net-worth individuals. The rich may have an incentive to form their own country to avoid paying the bulk of the cost of public goods for the rest of us. In the United States, the top 10 percent of wage earners pay over 70 percent of all taxes.[17] But the top 10 percent of wage earners are spread throughout the country. Given the dispersal of wealthy individuals, establishing a new state for multimillionaires is impractical. If the rich all lived in one place, there would be a much greater incentive to secede. By contrast, various ethnic groups may have clustered centuries ago in one part of a country. That explains why a vast majority of secession movements have been fought along ethnic divisions. (This is the equivalent of the existence of the second condition—limited migration post-partition—for the breakup of a nation with low up-front and ongoing costs.)

Additionally, many countries have high levels of ethnic diversity but no history of civil wars. Some of these countries even suffer from high levels of political exclusion of certain ethnic groups. But because ethnic groups are dispersed throughout a country, secession is geographically impractical. Moreover, a dispersed ethnic group that tries to establish a new ethnically homogeneous independent state is likely to be strongly resisted by the soon-to-be-displaced residents of that region in which the ethnic group intends to congregate.

There are also other reasons that civil wars tend to be fought along ethnic lines, independent of the level of ethnic diversity within a state. Ethnic minorities are more likely to be excluded from power by an ethnic majority. Ethnic groups also can enjoy greater cohesion, an important factor when fighting a rebellion that requires collective action against a strong central authority.

Hence, ethnic diversity is not the primary driver of civil wars. Rather, greater ethnic diversity is associated with countries that are more geographically segregated. But it is mainly geographical segregation, not ethnic diversity, that makes a nation more prone to secession. If all those in the United States worth more than $10 million resided on the island of Maui, then that tropical paradise might have already seceded from the Union. But if that were to happen, it would not mean that extreme income inequality necessarily leads to civil war. It just means that most rich people resided in the same region.

Another important factor is sharing a common border. Most nations that secede are not contiguous. Of the 124 new nations formed since World War II, only thirty-seven (30 percent) were contiguous to the old nation. Part of the reason is that decolonization was such a large part of the formation of new nations. However, this also demonstrates that resistance to secession is greater when the rebels are in close geographical proximity. If the former satellites of the Soviet Union are excluded, only 15 percent of new nations were formed out of contiguous states. In terms of secession, distance does not make the heart grow fonder. The more distant the nation, the less resistance to secession.

Equally importantly, in only 8 percent of the 124 new nations formed since World War II did secession trigger other secessions within the same country. Nations are reluctant to allow a region to secede if by granting permission to separate, other regions may follow. European nations fought hard against colonial independence for most of the nineteenth century and the first half of the twentieth century, and European leaders understood that granting even a single colony independence could lead to insurrections throughout their dominions. However, once these countries decided to decolonize, there was significantly less resistance to secession. Similarly, the Soviet Union brutally repressed dissent in its satellite nations for more than forty years. Soviet leaders understood that granting one nation independence threatened Russian control of every other subjugated country. But once the Soviets permitted Poland to rebel, other movements for independence immediately arose, and most Eastern Bloc countries were freed soon thereafter.

In the case of Czechoslovakia, the political leaders of that nation did not fear additional insurrections. By contrast, the leaders of Yugoslavia understood that secession by one region could lead to secession by all, as a weakened central government is more vulnerable to demands for independence by rebellious regions. They were right, and a bloody civil war ensued.

Hence, the splintering of nations often occurs in waves. When some European colonies sought independence before World War II, they were brutally repressed. European nations feared that the loss of one colony could lead to the loss of all. Similarly, the Soviet Union crushed the secession movements of every Eastern Bloc nation for four decades until it freed them all within a year.

We have seen that since World War II, the optimal size of a nation has steadily shrunk due to the impact of the five factors. Most of the new nations that have been formed came out of decolonization and the collapse of the Soviet Union. As our theory predicted, when the optimal size of states decreased and the pressure to partition mounted, those countries in which the up-front costs were the lowest were the first to separate.

Unfortunately, the next wave of partitions in the twenty-first century will likely be much more difficult. This trend is evident in the dissolution of Ethiopia, East Timor, Yugoslavia, and Sudan. The breakup of nations in which the two conditions for successful partition—pre-partition functioning states and limited migration post-partition—are not met have resulted in substantial losses of blood and treasure.

At the same time, geographical constraints have prevented many nations that are too small from expanding. Today, among the 196 sovereign states currently recognized by the United Nations, most are small, with 104 nations with a population of less than 10 million.[18] Within that group, there are thirty-seven island nations.[19] Surrounded by vast bodies of water, these countries are likely to forever remain too small. Other countries, such as Switzerland or Bhutan, are ringed by high mountain ranges and could not expand geographically as a practical matter, even if they wanted to.

Hence, the explosion in the number of countries since World War II can be explained by the optimal size of nations shrinking, pressuring many larger countries to partition, and geographic constraints, preventing many smaller countries from expanding.

Nevertheless, there remain a number of large nations that are still too big and continue to suffer political turmoil and internal strife. As we will see in the next chapter, for nations that are unwilling or unable to partition, there are two means to increase consensus: decentralize or establish a more authoritarian central government.

We will look at the latter first.

To illustrate, we return once last time to the 1860s and consider the counterfactual claim that the American Civil War could have been avoided if the United States had been a true democracy.

CHAPTER 9

DECENTRALIZATION AND AUTHORITARIANISM

MINORITY RULE IN SOUTH CAROLINA

The 1860 US Census recorded 402,406 slaves and 291,300 white people in South Carolina.[1] Slaves were also nearly a majority of the population in Louisiana and Alabama.[2] States in the South before the Civil War were able to survive because they were authoritarian regimes in which African Americans were enslaved, held captive by brute force. As the ruling minority or near minority in several states, white people perpetuated the institution of slavery through violence. If African Americans had been allowed to vote, South Carolina would have outlawed slavery. The same situation might have applied to other Southern states with large African-American populations, and the Civil War might have been avoided.

South Carolina and similar states offset a low level of consensus among their citizens with a high level of autocracy. Consensus measures the average difference between the preferences of the citizens of a state, including the preference not to be beaten or killed. Consensus does not gauge justice or morality; thus a government can achieve consensus among its people through punishments.

In the case of pre–Civil War South Carolina, the state and local governments used threats of violence to increase consensus, following a path common to most authoritarian regimes. Autocrats with absolute power over their subjects can force consensus, as the preference for most citizens is to avoid a painful death. African Americans trapped in the South before the Civil War had priorities that included staying alive.

In the context of authoritarianism, the word *optimal* is descriptive, not prescriptive. Optimal relates to the trade-offs between a state's size and consensus. All other things being equal, it is preferable to live in an optimal state. However, things are rarely equal. An autocrat can increase consensus with threats of punishment or death, while democracies have fewer tools at their disposal to increase consensus. Democracies wield incentives, but autocracies employ incentives *and* coercion, including oppressing a segment of the population through the use of violence. Hence, *the more democratic a government, the smaller the optimal size of a nation.*

THE POSITIVE FEEDBACK LOOP OF AUTOCRACY

Given the greater number of tools autocracies use to increase consensus, it is not surprising that autocracies have been the norm throughout most of human history. In addition, autocracies benefit from the fact that stronger central governments tend to become stronger over time.

Funding a government requires collecting taxes. If all citizens contribute, all benefit equally. If only a few contribute, then those who do not pay benefit from the payments of others. In the earliest tax-collecting states, central authorities were granted the right to use violence against their own citizens to make sure everyone paid their fair share. The greater the coercive power of the state, the more individuals who can be forced to pay. In turn, the more individuals who pay, the more coercive power a state can afford. For thousands of years, this has served as a positive feedback loop, leading to the rise of increasingly authoritarian states.[3] A stronger coercive central authority also meant that more monies could be extracted to fund a stronger military to conquer other states. Hence, in the evolutionary struggle between nations, those countries with stronger central authorities generally survived longer.

Over time, those who ran these strong central authorities soon realized they could extract most of the economic surplus for themselves. Within several thousand years after the start of the Agricultural Revolution, more than 90 percent of the world's population were peasants working the fields.[4] Of those working the land, roughly three-quarters were either indentured serfs or slaves.[5] The Egyptian pyramids were not built with unionized labor.

An account from eighth-century China tells of an alliance of local rulers and large landowners against peasant farmers: "The nobles, officials, and powerful local families set up their estates one next to the other, swallowing up peasants' lands as they please without fear of regulations. . . . They illegally buy the peasants' equal-field land. . . . They thus leave the peasants no place to live."[6]

The lack of consensus between the elites and the rest of the population was evidenced by the number of peasant uprisings during this time. In Europe, more than five hundred insurrections occurred between 1590 and 1715.[7] In feudal Japan, more than 1,800 peasant revolts are recorded between 1603 and 1868.[8] In China, one survey found 269 mass uprisings over a period of two thousand years.[9]

An account written in 1358, after a revolt in France, recalled the actions of peasants:

> *Going forth with their arms and standards, they overran the countryside. They killed, slaughtered and massacred without mercy all the nobles whom they could find, even their own lords. . . . They leveled the houses and fortresses of the nobles to the ground and . . . they delivered the noble ladies and their little children whom they came upon to an atrocious death.*[10]

To maintain consensus, agrarian states were authoritarian, with few exceptions. While everybody else was toiling in the fields, the rulers lived lavishly, building grand palaces and funding works of art, literature, and music for their own amusement. One study concluded that by as late as the time of the American Revolution, only 4 percent of the world's population was free—the rest were either slaves, serfs, vassals, or servants.[11]

But the extreme inequality that characterized these autocracies would not last. Despite the fierce battles waged by the agrarian elites to retain control of central authorities, the fundamental shifts in political and economic power brought on by the Industrial Revolution ushered in a new era of democracy.

INDUSTRIALIZATION AND
THE RISE OF DEMOCRACY

Until the Industrial Revolution, the amount of capital in the economy was largely fixed, as it was almost all land. The returns to capital accrued to the political and economic elites who owned most of the fields and farms. Since slavery in its many forms and peasant farming were the norm, workers tilled the soil for subsistence wages, and economic surpluses flowed to those at the top.

Starting with the Industrial Revolution and continuing until the present day, the amount of capital in the economy at any given time has varied, depending on market conditions and government tax policy. If central authorities attempt to grab most of the economic surplus, then the amount of investment and human capital contracts. If states impose draconian taxes, then the owners of capital either move their funds elsewhere or decide to consume rather than invest. If states levy excessive income taxes, then workers spend more time at leisure. The Industrial Revolution effectively capped the amount of economic surplus that political and economic elites could extract for themselves.

As a result, the Industrial Revolution transferred economic and political power to capitalists and workers who demanded new forms of government. Starting in the nineteenth and continuing through the twentieth century, democracy, communism, and fascism spread throughout the world. These systems were designed to replace the ruling agricultural autocracies with forms of government that were more responsive to the needs of industrialists and those who labored in their factories.

Under democracy, power resided with the workers through the ballot box, although election results could be influenced by funds contributed to political campaigns. Under communism and fascism, power was handed to a small group of political leaders, supposedly ruling on behalf of workers. In the end, communism and fascism failed, as the leaders of these forms of government acted much the same as the czars, emperors, and pharaohs who had come before. There remain some autocratic governments today, but most have retreated from controlling the everyday economic lives of workers, choosing instead to fight for continued political power and privilege.

In less than a century, the Industrial Revolution swept away the economic, political, and social structures of the Agricultural Revolution that had existed for thousands of years. In 1816, more than 90 percent of the world's population was living either in an authoritarian state or a colony.[12] Today, democracies outnumber authoritarian states.[13]

However, the distinction between democracies and autocracies is often blurred. In fact, these two terms are idealized notions. In the real world, nations exist on a continuum between these two extremes.

DEMOCRACY: A MATTER OF DEGREE

A democracy is a state in which decisions are made by majority vote. An autocracy is one in which decisions are made by a single individual. But democracies have historically not allowed everyone to vote.

The often idealized "democracies" of ancient Greece were not so democratic. The Greek city-states were authoritarian regimes governed by a ruling elite. Slaves made up two-thirds of the population in Plato's Athenian democracy.[14] In neighboring Sparta, it was an even higher percentage.[15] Slaves toiled in the mines, fields, and households, in what was considered the natural order. In Book 1 of *Politics*, Aristotle wrote on slavery and the nature of slaves:

> *Those who are as different [from other men] as the soul from the body or man from beast—and they are in this state if their work is the use of the body, and if this is the best that can come from them—are slaves by nature. For them it is better to be ruled in accordance with this sort of rule.*[16]

Greek slaves were considered property and treated as such. At one point in Athens, a mule was worth three slaves.[17] Female slaves of reproductive age were particularly prized as vessels to produce more slaves.[18]

English democracy began with the signing of the Magna Carta in 1215, but this was a peace treaty between the king and a handful of rebel barons. A later version in 1225 limited the power of the king in exchange for agreeing to pay taxes and became the basis for rule by consent in Western democracies. But at that time, only a small percentage of the adult male population was permitted to vote for Parliament, and slavery was legal. It was not until 1832 that suffrage was extended in England to any adult male who rented or owned land of a certain value. Slavery was outlawed only a year later. In 1918, the right to vote was extended to all males and some women who met certain qualifications, and, in 1928, to all women.

Democracies and autocracies exist on a continuum of voting rights. A democracy allows most citizens to participate in elections. But is a nation a democracy if only half of its citizens are allowed to vote? If the answer is yes, then what percentage of the population can be disenfranchised before the nation crosses over into an autocracy?

For most of its history, the United States has not been a true democracy by any measure.[19] Before the American Revolution, only white Christian property-owning men were enfranchised. Only an estimated 6 percent of the population was eligible to vote for President George Washington. Individual states determined who could vote, but in the decades that followed, the franchise was only expanded to include all white males. With the ratification of the Fourteenth Amendment in 1868 and the Fifteenth Amendment in 1870, African American males were granted citizenship and the right to vote, respectively, but Southern states effectively barred most Black citizens from the polls with literacy tests, taxes, and outright intimidation. In 1920 the passage of the Nineteenth Amendment granted all citizens the right to vote, and women across the nation participated in national elections for the first time.

However, the right to vote was not yet universal in the United States. African Americans throughout much of the South were still effectively disenfranchised, and Native Americans and Asians, many of whom were denied citizenship, could not gain access to the polls. In 1952, the McCarran-Walter Act granted Asian Americans citizenship. The Voting Rights Act of 1965 removed most of the remaining obstacles put up by many states to prevent people of color from voting. In 1971, the voting age was lowered from twenty-one to eighteen. On the continuum between autocracy and democracy, the United States did not cross over to the democratic side of that spectrum until the second half of the twentieth century.

Despite the overall trend toward more democratic governments across the globe over the course of the twentieth century, we have recently witnessed the rise to power of more authoritarian rulers in several large nations. For example, the governments of China and Russia have become more authoritarian during the twenty-first century (see Chapter 10). As a result, the optimal size of both these nations has increased over the past two decades.

This is part of the reason that both countries have become increasingly outwardly aggressive, threatening to occupy or annex neighboring nations. China has signaled that Taiwan may become part of the People's Republic of China sooner rather than later, regardless of the fact that most residents of that island favor independence. Russia invaded Georgia in 2008, effectively took over Crimea in 2014, and then attacked Ukraine again in 2022.

Throughout history, the transition to a more authoritarian regime has frequently been followed by attempts to conquer neighboring countries (see Germany and Japan in the 1930s). Of course, the decision to wage war is the product of many factors. But one of them is the establishment of a more authoritarian government which increases the optimal size of a nation and therefore provides an incentive to annex other nearby countries.

Living in an optimally sized country is good, all else being equal. But all else is rarely equal. I would rather live in a democracy that is too large than an autocracy that is of optimal size. Rather than place more political power in the hands of a few, a better approach to increase consensus is decentralization.

DECENTRALIZATION

To varying degrees, all nations decentralize the provision of government services. In political science, the idea of decentralizing public services is known as the subsidiarity principle: the central government should deliver only those public goods it is better at supplying than local governments. Under this principle a central government should provide national defense, while local governments should be responsible for police protection. A central government should set national air pollution standards, but it is up to local governments to regulate the dumping of waste into landfills.

The decentralization of public goods has an intuitive appeal. In theory, the governors can be held more accountable to the governed, or what has been called an "intimacy between the rulers and the ruled."[20] You are more likely to have your voice heard at a local school board meeting than at a session of the US House of Representatives. Decentralization allows government services to be tailored to meet the needs of local citizens, rather than employing a one-size-fits-all national approach. It also solves an agency problem common to all governments: The more centralized the collection of tax revenues, the more local government officials are motivated to please national leaders and ignore the wishes of local taxpayers.

Of course, not all government services should be supplied at the local level. The decision as to which level of government is best suited to deliver a particular public good has several considerations.

ECONOMIES OF SCALE AND SCOPE

The extent of economies of scale in the provision of public goods can differ widely.

As we discussed in Chapter 2, the provision of military forces is subject to significant economies of scale. That's one reason a larger and more populous state can fund defense forces at a lower cost per capita. Of course, some level of defense spending is necessary to survive in a hostile world. But the level of resources devoted to military forces is still constrained by the size of the nation. Hence, nations seek to leverage the economies of scale inherent in military forces by providing the public good with national defense at a national level.

By contrast, the provision of police forces has limited economies of scale. In fact, above the local level, there can be diseconomies of scale. In the United States, thousands of local and state police forces employ almost seven hundred thousand full-time law enforcement officers.[21] There is also a federal police force, known as the Federal Bureau of Investigation (FBI), staffed with roughly thirty-five thousand employees and a budget of more than $10 billion. The purpose of the FBI is mainly to pursue crimes that cross state lines. But if each state were a nation, there would be little need for the FBI. Instead, state police forces would work together, as other national police forces do through the International Criminal Police Organization, commonly known as Interpol. As an international police force, Interpol coordinates investigations and arrests across national borders for 194 member nations and is staffed with just over one thousand employees with an annual budget of 135 million euros.[22] This disparity between the cost of policing many states within a single nation and the cost of policing many countries illustrates that policing, above a certain level, suffers from diseconomies of scale. In the case of public safety, the central government does not have an advantage over local governments.

In addition to economies of scale, there are also economies of scope. In theory, one government providing many services is more efficient than many governments each supplying a few. The more levels of government, the greater the number of public officials. If the US federal government provided all public goods, then the nation would still bear the cost of one US president but save the expenses of fifty state governors.

While a greater scope of government decreases the number of elected officials, it also increases the number of administrators. To deliver services, a central government establishes local offices with regional managers. But someone has to manage the managers. By contrast, if a government service is delivered locally, then the top administrative layer of the central government is eliminated. Of course, for some government services, there is no local administration. For example, the provision of a national currency can be done most efficiently by a central bank.[23] But such examples are uncommon. The delivery of most government services requires a significant local administrative presence.

Reducing levels of administration through decentralization where possible can boost efficiency and responsiveness. More bureaucracy is not usually associated with better service. It is a fact that many public services just work better when performed locally. One centralized fire station for the entire nation would be a lot cheaper for taxpayers—but I suspect homeowners would have to pay higher premiums for fire insurance.

FORCING GOVERNMENTS TO COMPETE

Central governments enjoy a monopoly on the provision of many public goods. Unless a citizen is willing to emigrate, there is only one provider for nationwide government services. In the commercial sphere, a company that has gained a monopoly often charges too much for too little. The same is true for national governments.

Decentralization introduces a level of competition between governments. Local governments to some extent must compete for residents, or taxpayers may relocate. Of course, there are costs to moving and leaving friends and family behind. But the transition costs of moving cross-country are a lot less than immigrating to a new land with a different language and culture.

Competition also sparks innovation. A monopolist has less incentive to innovate than multiple companies struggling to gain market share. Similarly, competition between local governments encourages experimentation with new services and methods of funding and delivering those services. This innovation can be shared to enable local governments to adopt best practices from across the nation.

As in the private sector, competition does have downsides. In the public sector, there can be a "race to the bottom." An example is corporate charters. Companies in the United States incorporate based on state charters, which means that states compete to enact the most corporate-friendly laws to tempt companies to relocate. The winner in this particular race to the bottom has been Delaware, which boosts an extremely business-friendly set of corporate laws. Although no large US company has its headquarters or significant operations in Delaware, almost all large US companies call Delaware their corporate home. Similarly, regions compete for the relocation of factories by offering incentives, usually in the form of reduced taxes or outright subsidies. Decentralization forces local governments to compete for businesses. This competition can end up benefiting businesses at the expense of local communities and the nation as a whole.

MORAL HAZARD

Another advantage of decentralization is that the presence of a strong central government may encourage local governments to take unwise risks. For example, several large US states, such as California and Illinois, have committed to large pensions and other obligations they do not have the ability to pay.

But a bankruptcy of either California or Illinois would have significant economic consequences for the United States. It is therefore likely the US federal government would rescue these states, if it ever became necessary, because California and Illinois are "too big to fail." This moral hazard can encourage reckless behavior by local governments to promise more than they can deliver. In the worst-case scenario, states know that they can offload their pension and other obligations to the federal government. In 1975, the federal government bailed out New York City, providing $2.3 billion in direct loans, and then had to do it again in 1978 by guaranteeing $1.65 million of the city's debt obligations.[24]

SPILLOVER EFFECTS

While decentralization has many advantages, it is not a panacea. Spillover effects present a major drawback to decentralization.

An example is air pollution. Suppose a state has two regions, one with strict air pollution standards and another that allows companies to pollute at will. The region with the strict standards is in effect subsidizing the region with lax standards. The region with lax standards therefore has less incentive to restrict pollution, and the region with strict environmental standards does not receive the full benefit of monies spent to clean up the skies. Therefore, both regions have less incentive to spend taxpayer dollars on the public good of improved air quality.

Another example is military spending. If a nation is sandwiched between two friendly countries with strong military forces, there is less risk of a hostile nation invading the landlocked country. The strength of the militaries of the friendly neighboring countries benefits the sandwiched state. Luxembourg has less incentive to fund NATO since France and Germany are members. Luxembourg spends 0.5 percent of its GDP on defense, well below the 2 percent required by NATO membership and one of the lowest percentages of all NATO nations.[25]

As these examples illustrate, spillover effects result in one nation getting "free stuff" at the expense of another. The result is in the underfunding of public goods.

BEYOND ECONOMICS: MORE FREEDOM

Decentralization does have a significant advantage that goes beyond economic considerations: greater protection of personal liberty.

Governments are granted the right to employ coercion to ensure that citizens pay their fair share for public goods. These powers of coercion can be used for good—or evil. The more power and control given to local governments, the less the ability of an oppressive central government to persecute its citizens. An oppressive local government would face an exodus of residents to other parts of the country. Citizens can vote with their feet.

Decentralization of government also can allow for more personal freedoms. The provision of abortion services is an issue with strongly held beliefs on both sides. The Supreme Court ruled in 2022 that the provision of abortion services was up to individual states. As a result, some effectively prohibited the procedure, and others continued to permit it. In this case, a degree of decentralization compared with a federal ban on abortions offers more freedom of choice, as women can travel to a state that offers abortion services. Of course, this unfairly places a greater burden on those without the financial resources to travel out of state and take time off from work. However, for those seeking abortion services, at least some degree of choice is better than no choice at all. But if the Supreme Court were to ban all abortions, millions of women would be stripped of their personal liberties.

In general, I believe the advantages of greater freedoms and forcing governments to compete outweigh the disadvantages of the potential moral hazard and spillover effects from greater decentralization. Therefore, in states that are too big, the burden of proof should be on those who espouse authoritarianism to demonstrate why decentralization is not the better solution.

Unfortunately, the first two decades of the twenty-first century have witnessed the steady rise of authoritarianism. The American think tank Freedom House reported that seventy-three nations had a lower "freedom score" in 2020 than the year before.[26] Only twenty-eight nations saw their scores rise.[27] A Pew survey of twenty-three countries showed that the share of those nations where a majority liked "American ideas about democracy" fell from 58 percent to 35 percent from 2002 to 2017.[28]

In the final chapter, we will look at four large nations and consider the options for rightsizing those nations. Rather than decentralize, two of those nations, Russia and China, have transitioned over the past two decades to more authoritarian central governments.

- - - - - - - - - - - - - - -

CHAPTER 10

JAPAN, RUSSIA, CHINA, AND THE UNITED STATES

O f the twenty-five most populous nations on the planet, four in particular—Japan, Russia, China, and the United States—currently face tough trade-offs between size and consensus. In examining how these countries have been affected by the five factors, I will look at what steps, if any, they could take to become optimally sized.

I am confident that some readers will disagree with some (or all) of my conclusions. In my defense, I lived in three of the four countries (United States, Japan, and China) for multiple years at different periods during my adult life. But reasonable people may differ about whether these nations are too small, too big, or optimally sized.

JAPAN

The Japanese nation developed from a mix of loyalty to an imperial line dating from the seventh century BCE, Chinese Buddhism that swept the nation during the sixth century CE, and the Indigenous culture that emerged during the Heian period (794–1185), anchored in the Shinto religion and celebrated in a rich literary and artistic tradition.

As an island stranded in the northwestern Pacific Ocean, Japan experienced irregular contact with others throughout most of its history. The unique character of Japan fully emerged during the Edo period (1603–1868) when the nation was closed to foreigners. It was not until Commodore Matthew Perry steamed into Edo Bay in 1853 and forcibly opened the nation that outside influences began to once again seep into Japan. By that time, hundreds of years of isolation had given the Japanese a strong sense of national identity that continues to this day. Japan is unique among the large, developed nations of the modern world in that non-Indigenous influences did not cross its borders until the second half of the nineteenth century.

Japan has been a remarkable success story. Less than one-third of the land on the Japanese islands is habitable, due to steep mountain ranges.[1] There are virtually no natural resources—80 percent of oil is imported[2]—and agriculture is severely limited, with 60 percent of its food shipped in from overseas.[3] Plus, in 1945, the nation's industrial infrastructure was left in rubble from US bombing, and most houses within the major cities had burned to the ground after the raging firestorms. The Japanese had to rebuild their country from the ground up seventy-seven years ago. Yet Japan, with 125 million people, is the third largest economy in the world, only recently surpassed by China, which has a population of 1.4 billion.

In terms of the incidence of war, Japan is at greater risk than ever before from aggression from a newly powerful and rich China. The People's Republic of China (PRC) is in the process of building a vast navy to eventually push the US Navy out of the waters off the east coast of China. Once that happens, China could easily blockade Japan, which depends on imports for most of its food and fuel. In its long history, Japan has never been confronted by an aggressive Asian neighbor with a substantially more powerful military that could place a stranglehold on the island nation. The growing risk of armed conflict with China will increase the optimal size of Japan in the years ahead.

In terms of the cost of national defense, Japan has benefited from the protection of a nuclear umbrella extended across the Pacific by the United States. Consequently, Japan has historically spent less than 1 percent of its GDP on military forces. But it is unclear whether the United States would risk nuclear war to save Japan. Would the US government trade Seattle for Tokyo? If the US nuclear umbrella is withdrawn, the cost of Japan's national defense will substantially rise, also increasing the optimal size of Japan.

In terms of income inequality, Japan has less income inequality than that of any nation on earth. According to the United Nations, the ratio of the average income of the richest 10 percent in Japan to the poorest 10 percent is lower than that of all other countries.[4] The same ratio for wealth is also the lowest.[5] For comparison, as of 2020, the wealth share of the top 10 percent in Japan and the United States was 18 percent and 35 percent, respectively.[6] Relatively little income inequality further increases the optimal size of Japan.

Japan also enjoys a high level of internal consensus. The nation has an extreme level of homogeneity, as 98 percent of the nation is of Japanese descent.[7] The Japanese language is universally written and spoken. Japan has not suffered from the recent cultural wars of other developed countries in the West. Furthermore, there is general agreement within Japan about public policy. Unlike the United States, the two major Japanese political parties basically hold the same views. Prime ministers come and go, but the bureaucrats who run the country day to day from the various ministries remain in place. In addition, the population of Japan has been rapidly aging and falling. The total population is projected to decline from 125 million in 2015 to 88 million in 2065.[8] In general, fewer people should result in fewer disagreements.

Hence, Japan is too small and becoming smaller with each passing day. To become an optimally sized state, Japan has several options, but none of them seem feasible.

Japan could open its doors to millions of young immigrant families to grow its population. This is unlikely. Immigration to Japan is strictly limited, with only an estimated sixty thousand people living there without official permission.[9] Only several thousand requests for Japanese citizenship are granted each year, after a rigorous and lengthy interview process, including fluency tests.[10]

Japan could use its wealth to offer massive subsidies to another country to surrender its sovereignty. However, as an island nation, the gains in economies of scale in delivering public goods from annexing another country would likely be less than the costs of generous subsidies. In any case, I doubt that even in years past the response to such an offer would have been favorable. Definitely not now, as Japan's neighbors (South Korea, Taiwan, Philippines) have recently gotten wealthy. The current ruler of North Korea does not seem to be willing at any price to surrender his sovereignty.

In my view, Japan is likely to stay too small or become even smaller.

RUSSIA

Russia has been and continues to be more of an autocracy than a democracy.

Nominally, Russian rulers are selected by popular vote, but Vladimir Putin was elected president in 2000 and subsequently has consolidated his political power over the Russian military, media, and most of the nation's largest companies. Putin's "reelections" have been anything but free.

But this is not new. Except for a brief period after the fall of the Iron Curtain, Russia has been ruled by autocrats for more than seven centuries. It began with the Tartars in the Middle Ages and was followed by a succession of tsars, and later Lenin, Stalin, and a series of general secretaries of the Communist Party. Putin is the latest in a long line of Russian strongmen.

For more than five centuries before the founding of the Russian Empire, the people of Russia shared a common language and culture, a combination of Slavic and Byzantine influences. The Slavs are the largest ethnic group in Europe, descended from tribes that populated Eurasia. The Slavs spoke Proto-Slavic, the language that evolved into modern Russian. Most Russians also have shared a common religion throughout the nation's history. In 987, Vladimir the Great adopted Orthodox Christianity, the religion of the Byzantine Empire, as the official state religion. The Russian Orthodox Church would go on to survive another thousand years, including almost a century of communism, and today remains an important part of Russian everyday life. Despite the repression of religion during the Soviet era, most Russians today consider themselves believers,[11] and the Orthodox Church serves as the de facto state religion.

The countries of the Soviet Eastern Bloc did not share this heritage. In fact, Eastern Bloc countries viewed themselves as part of Europe and enjoyed their own distinct national languages, such as German, Czech, Slovak, Polish, Hungarian, and Romanian. Like most European nations, the predominant religions in the Eastern Bloc countries were Catholicism and Protestantism, at odds with the Orthodox Christianity that permeated Russian culture.[12]

Nevertheless, the Soviets after World War II were able to achieve the greatest expansion of the Russian state in the nation's history. But the occupation of Eastern Europe resulted in a Soviet state that was too big. In the end, Russia was forced to return to its pre–World War II borders encompassing the traditional Slavic homeland.

In terms of the incidence of war and cost of national defense, Russia has had little to fear from its European neighbors. During the nineteenth and twentieth centuries, Napoleon and Hitler were real threats to the Russian state as their armies marched across the broad, flat plain of Eastern Europe deep into Russian territory. There is no such danger from NATO. To date, China has demonstrated no interest in taking over Russia's barren eastern lands. In addition, the cost of nuclear and biological weapons has decreased over the same period due to advances in technology. Hence, the optimal size of Russia has shrunk since the fall of the Berlin Wall and with the overall decline in incidence of war and threats from European nations.

Russia clearly suffers from income inequality, and much of

Russian income and wealth is undisclosed and held overseas, out of the reach of tax authorities. The "black market" economy is also a significant part of the gross national product. The combination of these two factors limits the ability of the regime to implement transfer payments from those with the most to those with the least, even if the plutocratic Russian leadership decided to do so. Therefore, rising income inequality is also shrinking the size of the Russia state.

At the same time the optimal size of Russia is declining, the nation is suffering from a growing xenophobia and a fear of chaos, both of which are powerful forces that have united the Russian people. Russians hold highly unfavorable views of the West and particularly distrust the Chinese.[13] Most Russians support a degree of authoritarianism. A 2020 survey revealed that 75 percent of Russians want their country to be ruled by a "strong and powerful leader."[14] Despite criticism in the West, Putin has the support of most Russians.[15]

During the twenty-first century, Russia has become even more of an authoritarian state. Putin has consolidated power over the Duma (the lower house of the Russian Federal Assembly), his allies control most major industries, and his surrogates almost all media. In 2020, the Russian constitution was amended to allow Putin to continue to be president until 2036, when he will be eighty-four years old, based on a national referendum that has been described as a "fake and massive lie."[16] Putin has imprisoned leading opposition leaders and allegedly had others killed or made attempts on their lives. In 2014, the Russian deputy chief of staff said, "There is no Russia today if there is no Putin."[17] In addition, the population of Russia is rapidly aging, predicted to fall from 145 million in 2020 to 126 million by 2100.[18]

As Putin's power grows and the Russian population contracts, Russia will become even smaller, pushing the nation to grow in size. This is one reason that Russia has become more outwardly aggressive. In 2008, Russia invaded Georgia and then, in 2014, annexed Crimea. In 2022, Russia attacked Ukraine.

CHINA

The Chinese Empire has survived for more than two thousand years, based on the continuity of the Han civilization. The Han dynasty united the Chinese people around the core principles set out by Confucius, a secular morality built on filial loyalty and ancestor worship as well as harmonious relationships between individuals. Although succeeded by a long line of other dynastic rulers, the Han emperors established the language, customs, and culture that continue to resonate throughout China today. Most Chinese identify more strongly with Han culture than with any political ideology, despite almost three-quarters of a century of communist rule.

Since the establishment of the People's Republic of China (PRC) in 1949, China has been ruled by one party, the Chinese Communist Party (CCP). During this time, the optimal size of the Chinese state has been steadily shrinking.

In terms of the incidence of warfare and national defense, there have been no real threats to the sovereignty or territories of the PRC, post the flight of Chiang Kai-shek to Taiwan. The nation that posed the greatest threat to China in the first half of the twentieth century was Japan, and that country was effectively pacified after World War II. By the late 1960s, although still poor, China was able to design and deploy nuclear and biological weapons to deter attacks on its homeland. A combination of a more peaceful world in general, a more peaceful Japan in particular, and the acquisition of weapons of mass destruction reduced the optimal size of the Chinese state.

In terms of international trade, the PRC was largely cut off from the rest of the world during the latter half of the twentieth century. That all changed in 2001 when the PRC entered the WTO after fifteen years of negotiations. There has been much debate on the extent to which the PRC in practice adheres to the spirit and letter of WTO agreements. The PRC imposes capital controls, manages currency fluctuations, subsidizes domestic state-owned enterprises, and has yet to establish a level playing field in the Chinese courts for domestic and foreign companies, particularly concerning intellectual property. Nevertheless, trade barriers with the rest of the world, at least in terms of other countries opening their domestic markets to China, have declined significantly. Thus, greater opportunities to access foreign markets have also served to shrink the optimal size of the Chinese state.

In terms of income inequality, the chasm between the haves and have-nots in China has widened since World War II. From 1978 to 2015, the share of public property in national wealth fell from approximately 70 percent to 30 percent.[19] During this period, the PRC privatized much of the housing stock: Today, 95 percent of homes are held by private individuals, compared to about 50 percent in 1978.[20] About one-third of publicly traded companies are now owned by individuals, up from close to 0 percent during the 1960s.[21] While reliable statistics on the distribution of private property are not available, it is generally believed that wealth is heavily concentrated within Chinese economic and political elites. Furthermore, the share of national income earned by the top 10 percent from the 1970s to today rose from 27 percent to 41 percent.[22] By all accounts, wealth and income inequality have risen in the last half century, further reducing the optimal size of the Chinese nation.

The factors reducing the optimal size of the Chinese state—a lower incidence of war, more access to foreign markets, greater income inequality—have been compounded in the last several decades by an increasingly autocratic regime. During the 1970s, Deng Xiaoping, as chairman of the CCP, launched a series of reforms, relaxing economic controls, which fueled an economic expansion, and China replaced Japan as the second largest economy in the world. Hundreds of millions of people moved to the cities and were lifted out of poverty. However, the central government has subsequently brutally repressed protests, such as the Tiananmen demonstrations in 1989 and those in Hong Kong in 2019–2020. Dissidents have been detained, journalists silenced, and internet access restricted.

More recently, China has become even more authoritarian due to the consolidation of power under one man—Xi Jinping. In 2016, Xi set himself up as "chairman for life" of the CCP, appointing himself head of the Politburo Standing Committee and Central Military Commission. He has vanquished his rivals and appears determined to further consolidate his power, steadily replacing members of these two bodies, which effectively rule China, with his allies. Xi, who turned sixty-nine years old in 2022, is set to rule for decades to come. He is the most powerful Chinese leader since Mao Zedong.

The rise of a greater authoritarian rule under Xi is partly because if China were to switch to a democratic form of government, the country would be too big.

Although China annexed Hong Kong in 1997, the residents of the former British colony are overwhelmingly against being part of the PRC. Many pro-democracy politicians have fled into exile or languish in mainland jails. Local news media has been censored. A new security law allows for the arrest of any Hong Kong resident for basically any reason. In June 2019, an estimated one million Hong Kong Chinese took to the streets to protest mainland rule. A violent crackdown followed, accompanied by threats that the People's Liberation Army would occupy the former colony if the unrest continued.

In response, many Hong Kong citizens are fleeing. The PRC restricts publication of independently verified population data concerning Hong Kong. However, the exodus of Hong Kong Chinese is evidenced by a report that in 2021, HK$1.9 billion was pulled out of the Mandatory Provident Fund, the equivalent of social security in the United States, as people moved overseas.[23]

China also represses ethnic minorities. Two examples are the Uighurs and Tibetans. A UN report found that Uighurs in the Xinjiang Uighur Autonomous Region are subject to "systematic repression," including "arbitrary, prolonged and incommunicado mass detention."[24] The subjugation of Tibet has been widely reported. Either of these ethnic minorities, if given an opportunity, would immediately embrace independence.

With the consolidation of Xi's power, the nation has become more outwardly aggressive. Xi has begun to lay the groundwork for the annexation of Taiwan, although the residents of that island have little interest in PRC rule.[25] In recent years, the PRC has regularly sent fighter planes into Taiwanese airspace to test national defense capabilities.[26] In early 2022, when Russia attacked Ukraine, China refused to call it an invasion, anticipating that the same could be said of China during a future takeover of Taiwan.[27]

Nevertheless, there is a widespread consensus among Han Chinese citizens, who represent 94 percent of the mainland's population. There is a particularly high level of consensus within this group compared with other large countries.[28] A recent survey by an independent US research firm found that 95 percent of Han Chinese citizens were either "relatively satisfied" or "highly satisfied" with the direction the central government was taking the nation.[29] (By comparison, the same survey found that only 38 percent of Americans felt that way about their country.)[30] Another survey reported that 93 percent of Chinese would opt for security over freedom, if forced to choose.[31] This compares with only about half of respondents choosing security over freedom in Western countries.[32]

In my view, China is too small. But that is only because of authoritarian rule by the CCP. If the CCP were to allow self-determination, several regions would likely immediately secede. And Taiwan would have nothing to fear. If China were a true democracy, it would be too big.

As Xi's power increases, China will become even smaller, driving its leaders to annex neighboring countries, such as Taiwan.

THE UNITED STATES

The United States has been suffering from increasing levels of political turmoil and internal strife. A Pew Research Center poll showed that the political polarization between Republicans and Democrats doubled between 1978 and 2019.[33] From 1960 to 2008, Americans were twice as likely to think members of the other party were more selfish than they were and eight times more likely to believe members of the opposing party were less intelligent.[34] In 1960, 5 percent of Americans reported they would be upset if their child married someone from the other political party. By 2010, that number was more than 40 percent.[35]

Of course, there have been periods in our history when Americans were even more at odds with one another. In the late eighteenth century, there was armed conflict between those who favored independence from Great Britain and the Royalists who wished to remain part of the British Empire. There was a wide political and cultural chasm between Democrats in the South and Republicans in the North in the decades leading up to and following the Civil War. During these periods of American history, the political and cultural gulf between partisans was even greater than what exists today.

Nevertheless, while not comparable to the most divisive periods in our nation's history, the split between liberals and conservatives has significantly widened. That split is primarily geographical. More Americans than ever are living in what analysts call "landslide counties," defined as those in which the winning presidential candidate received more than 60 percent of the vote. In 1992, 39 percent of voters lived in landslide counties.[36] By 2016, that number was 61 percent.[37]

In fact, population density is the most reliable indicator of party allegiance. The median population density for the average Democrat is 1,197 people per square mile, compared with 585 per square mile for the average Republican.[38] Counties with more than 800 people per square mile are almost always Democratic and those that are less densely populated are almost always Republican.[39] In 2016, Donald Trump garnered a greater number of votes than Hillary Clinton in 2,584 of the nation's 3,056 counties.[40] But those counties that Trump won represented only 45 percent of the nation's population.[41] It was Clinton's overwhelming wins in many of the nation's most populous counties that earned her more popular votes. In 2020, Trump won 2,547 counties compared to 509 for Joe Biden.[42] Biden won the presidency based on the urban vote. It's Priuses versus pickups.[43]

As divisions between the two major political parties have been growing, how have the five factors been affecting the optimal size of the United States?

In terms of the incidence of war and cost of national defense, the Long Peace since World War II has produced a sharp decline in military conflicts. The cost of national defense has been steadily falling since the end of World War II, shrinking the optimal size of the United States.

In terms of international trade, the United States has been the strongest proponent of the WTO. International trade has steadily increased during the twenty-first century, as global supply chains have been extended throughout the world. Although the United States imposed tariffs on some Chinese goods and bans on Russian oil in response to recent actions taken by those countries, the United States has enjoyed greater access to most foreign markets with each passing decade, reducing the benefits of a large domestic market for goods and services.

In terms of income inequality, the United States has experienced a growing gap between the rich and poor, much like around the world in general. With an increase in artificial intelligence and other technological developments, I expect income inequality to continue to rise, absent significant changes to tax policy. Furthermore, NATO and the WTO have been effective IGOs, which has further decreased the advantages of a larger country.

Hence, all five factors that affect the optimal size of a nation—incidence of warfare, cost of national defense, international trade, income inequality, and the existence of effective IGOs—have been shrinking the optimal size of the United States. This in a nation that is increasingly politically divided.

The decreased optimal size of the United States could be offset by decentralization or partition. Both are powerful remedies for the ills that can plague a nation that is too big. Unfortunately, in the case of the United States, I don't think either decentralization or partition will work.

America is geographically divided into Democrats and Republicans but not regionally. Democratic Priuses and Republican pickups criss-cross every state. For example, Illinois is solidly Democratic. In 2020, Biden received 3.4 million votes compared with Trump's 2.4 million. While Chicago and the surrounding metropolitan area are over-whelmingly Democratic, the rest of the state is largely Republican. In Cook County, home to Chicago, 74 percent of voters cast ballots for Biden.[44] In downstate Wayne County, 84 percent of residents supported Trump.[45] Texas is similarly politically divided between urban and rural communities. In 2020, Trump garnered 5.9 million votes to Biden's 5.2 million. In Dallas County, Biden won 65 percent of the vote.[46] In rural Hardin County, Trump won 86 percent.[47] The twenty-two Texas counties that Biden won included the five most populous, while the other 232 counties went to Trump.[48]

Decentralization would transfer the provision of many public goods from the federal to the state governments. In addition, reso-lution of contentious issues such as abortion and gun rights could be left to the individual states. But many states, such as Illinois and Texas, are not uniformly Democratic or Republican. Hence, decentralization by pushing the provision of public goods and resolution of contentious issues down to the state level is unlikely to significantly raise the level of consensus within the country.

America could also be partitioned into two or more new sovereign nations that are Democratic and Republican. Unfortunately, the result of such a split would likely be a mass migration post-partition.

To avoid a mass migration, the United States would need to somehow be partitioned between urban and rural communities. Let's look at Illinois again. There's heavily Democratic Chicago and solidly Republican everywhere else in the state. In theory, two nations—Chicago and Everywhere Else—could be formed out of the existing state. This split would meet our criteria for a successful partition: There would be no mass migration, and the existing governments—the city of Chicago and the state of Illinois (less the Chicago representatives)—could rule their respective domains. But this would not be a great solution for everyone. For example, the city of Champaign in southern Illinois, home to University of Illinois Urbana-Champaign, is heavily Democratic and would be a blue island in a sea of red.

It is true that Americans are some of the most restless individuals on the planet. Approximately 10 percent of Americans move each year, and the average American moves eleven times in their lifetime.[49] Fifty-eight percent of Americans reside outside of the state in which they were born.[50] Most younger Americans naturally expect to transition from one state to another, leaving home for school and then school for a job. Later in life, career moves are still common. Nevertheless, a partition of the country would spark unplanned moves for many and would mean leaving family and friends behind. Careers would be upended, businesses sold or even abandoned. The disruption of personal and professional lives for tens of millions of people would be substantial.[51]

Regardless, dividing the country into dozens if not hundreds of sovereign entities, such as the new nations of Chicago and the Rest of Illinois, would likely result in countries that are too small. The loss of economics of scale in the provision of public goods, such as national defense and a common currency, would probably not justify the gain in consensus. In fact, such a partition could intensify the conflict between Americans, as the new, ideologically pure city-states and rural kingdoms could wage bitter partisan wars with newly formed militias.

A partition that would meet the criteria for a successful partition would be the secession of California, a state that is overwhelmingly Democratic. If California were to somehow leave the Union, there would unlikely be a mass migration, and the existing executive, legislative, and judicial branches of the California state government could take over the current functions of the US federal government, with the exception of national defense. But California could exploit the spillover effects (see Chapter 9) from sharing a continent defended by the US military, which would not allow a hostile foreign country to occupy an independent California and gain a platform from which to launch an invasion of the rest of the country. But the savings from exploiting the spillover effects from the public good of national defense is not the only reason for California to secede.

As we discussed in Chapter 5, California is a donor state, sending billions of dollars more each year in taxes to the federal government than it receives in transfer payments. As an independent nation, California could cut taxes and maintain the same level of government benefits and services. California voters are also disenfranchised. The state has a population of thirty-nine million and fifty-five Electoral College votes, while Wyoming has about a half million residents and three Electoral College votes. That means it takes 4.25 Californians to equal the vote of one Wyoming resident in US presidential elections. In the US Senate, the ballots of seventy-eight Californians receive the same weight as one Wyoming resident. The US Electoral College and US Senate heavily favor the more Republican states, which has implications for all branches of government. The US Supreme Court today has a solid majority of six of nine conservative justices, yet the Democratic Party has won the national popular vote for US president in seven of the last eight elections. On issues such as gun control, abortion, health care, and vaccine mandates, the rulings of a conservative US Supreme Court will impact the lives of liberal Californians for decades to come.

Numerous proposals for independence, including several ballot initiatives, have been put forward. The proponents of "Calexit" contend rightly that California is large enough to stand on its own as a nation. If California were a country, it would be the fifth largest economy in the world and the thirty-seventh most populous nation. After independence, California could implement a range of social programs that would be quite popular within the state, such as a single-payer health care system, various climate accords, and strict gun control laws. These are social programs that are all equally unpopular in some other parts of the country.

But Calexit would profoundly impact American politics. Without California, the Democratic Party would be in the minority in the US House and Senate, and the US president would be a Republican for decades to come.

Hence, Calexit would likely prompt the nearby and heavily Democratic states of Oregon and Washington to merge with the new California nation. Without California, Oregon, and Washington, Republicans would then have unfettered, complete control of the remaining US nation. If the West Coast left the Union, the liberal East Coast states would likely find it intolerable to remain. Led by New York, the New England states would likely seek independence. The domino effect of Calexit would be virtually unstoppable. Alternatively, if Calexit caused the secession of the eastern states, then Oregon and Washington would likely follow for similar reasons. Secession by any of the large blue states would so tilt the political balance within the country that other blue states would surely follow.

In the end, many states would likely oppose Calexit. The other blue states would vehemently object, concerned about their fate as a minority in the remaining Republican-dominated country. All states would suffer a reduction in the economies of scale in the delivery of public goods. Many states would then lose the billions of donor funds transferred each year from California. More than anything else, most Americans would rightly be fearful of the unforeseen consequences of the largest and wealthiest state leaving the Union.

Admittedly, a few red states would bid California a fond farewell. But most states would probably view Calexit as a disaster for the great American experiment in democracy. National political leaders would also realize that the departure of California could have a cascading effect that would shatter the Union, and so they would likely oppose secession and the resulting loss of employment. In my view, there is no middle ground: The United States either stays together or Calexit shatters the Union.

Consequently, if California attempted to secede, the other states would likely demand that the federal government forcibly put down the insurrection. This would require the US military to occupy parts of the Golden State. Such an action would grant the US president tremendous powers as commander-in-chief and establish an authoritarian federal government.

But Calexit is not the only event that could trigger the transfer of extraordinary powers to the executive branch of the federal government.

Imagine a revolt by a fiercely conservative Western town initially led by thousands of heavily armed local men, which is then joined by thousands of others with similar convictions (and weapons) from around the country. America has sixty-seven million more guns than people, about 1.2 firearms per resident, twice the ratio of the next highest nation, the civil war–torn Yemen.[52] But guns are unequally distributed: the average gun owner in the United States possesses eight firearms.[53] Such a revolt would likely be more than the local National Guard could (or would be willing to) put down and thus require deploying the US military.

If this insurrection ended in the deaths of thousands of American civilians at the hands of the US military, similar uprisings could spread to other conservative strongholds. In such a national crisis, Americans would demand order above all else, which would again result in granting the US president extraordinary powers, setting off even more protests and armed uprisings throughout the country. Some conservative states could threaten to leave the Union, sparking the reverse process of Calexit, in which Republican states fear being left behind in a nation that is overwhelmingly Democratic.

For these reasons, a nation that is too large, such as the United

States, is at greater risk to the establishment of an authoritarian government. When fighting takes to the streets, the reaction of most is to grant the necessary powers to the executive branch to reestablish peace. In a 2020 study, researchers found that the more US voters feel threatened by others, the more they are willing to grant greater powers to the central government and support authoritarian leaders.[54] The demands on the US president to restore order would be accompanied by expanding his powers to quash current and future rebellions.

In my view, the recent rise of politicians with authoritarian tendencies in the United States is an early warning sign. So too are the events at the US Capitol on January 6, 2021. In a bitterly divided nation in which both sides believe compromise impossible, one side may try to impose its will on the other.

If decentralization and partition are determined to be unworkable, the United States may follow the path of Russia and China and establish a more authoritarian central government in the years to come.

EPILOGUE

The factors that determine the optimal size of nations—the incidence of war, cost of national defense, free trade, income inequality, and effective IGOs—have been shrinking the optimal size of most countries since World War II. Hence, the explosion in the number of nations from seventy-four in 1945 to 196 in 2022.

These new nations that have arisen out of partition have generally met the two criteria for secession: pre-partition functioning governments and limited migration post-partition. Those nations that were too big and could partition with minimal up-front and ongoing costs have almost all done so. What remains are nations that are too big, but in which partition is unpractical or the perceived benefits of size outweigh the costs.

These countries are now confronted by difficult choices.

If partition is not an option, then the remaining choices are to continue with the status quo, decentralize, or transition to a more authoritarian government. Maintaining the status quo will likely result in decades of spiraling domestic strife, poisoned politics, and periodic outbreaks of secession movements and the risk of civil war. Decentralization leaves central governments in place and therefore only partly rightsizes a nation that is too big. However, decentralization often is unworkable for the same reasons countries do not partition. A transition to a more authoritarian regime for many nations is the only remaining choice and the path of least resistance.

The twentieth century was marked by great tragedy, such as two world wars that killed more than eighty million soldiers and civilians, and great triumphs, such as decolonization and the collapse of the Soviet Union, which granted hundreds of millions of people their political freedom.[1]

The first two decades of the twenty-first century have seen the rise of more authoritarian regimes in two of the world's largest nations, China and Russia. More authoritarian leaders also have risen to power in Europe (Turkey, Hungary, Slovenia), Africa (Chad, Mali, Sudan), the Americas (Bolivia, Venezuela), and Asia (Myanmar, Afghanistan). A study by the International Institute for Democracy and Electoral Assistance concluded, "Authoritarianism advances in every corner of the Earth. . . . The number of countries moving in an authoritarian direction in 2020 outnumbered those going in a democratic direction."[2] The authors warned that this report "is not a wakeup call, it's an alarm bell."[3]

I believe one of the most difficult challenges our generation will confront is the rise of authoritarianism in nations that are too big. Alarm bells are sounding in countries across Europe, Asia, Central and South America, and Africa. An alarm bell is now also ringing in the United States with the rise of populist, authoritarian leaders.

The twentieth century witnessed the triumph of democracy. Those gains are now at risk.

APPENDIX

The following chart lists new nations formed since 1945. Countries are sorted by the former larger nation of which they were a part, followed by the year partition was officially recognized.

D = Decolonization
S = Breakup of Soviet Union
O = Other not D or S

New Nation	Old Nation	Year of Partition	Type of Partition
Burundi	Belgium	1962	D
Congo	Belgium	1960	D
Rwanda	Belgium	1962	D
Czech Republic	Czechoslovakia	1993	O
Slovakia	Czechoslovakia	1993	O
Eritrea	Ethiopia	1993	D

continued

New Nation	Old Nation	Year of Partition	Type of Partition
Algeria	France	1962	D
Benin	France	1960	D
Burkina Faso	France	1960	D
Cambodia	France	1953	D
Cameroon	France	1960	D
Central African Republic	France	1960	D
Chad	France	1960	D
Comoros	France	1960	D
Côte d'Ivoire	France	1960	D
Djibouti	France	1977	D
Gabon	France	1960	D
Guinea	France	1958	D
Laos	France	1975	D
Madagascar	France	1960	D
Mali	France	1960	D
Mauritania	France	1960	D
Niger	France	1960	D
Senegal	France	1960	D
Syria	France	1946	D
Togo	France	1960	D

New Nation	Old Nation	Year of Partition	Type of Partition
Tunisia	France	1956	D
East Timor	Indonesia	2002	O
Palestine	Israel	1988	O
Libya	Italy	1951	D
Singapore	Malaysia	1965	O
Indonesia	Netherlands	1949	D
Suriname	Netherlands	1975	D
Samoa	New Zealand	1962	D
Bangladesh	Pakistan	1971	D
Angola	Portugal	1975	D
Cabo Verde	Portugal	1975	D
Guinea-Bissau	Portugal	1974	D
Mozambique	Portugal	1975	D
São Tomé/Principe	Portugal	1975	D
Namibia	South Africa	1990	D
Albania	Soviet Union	1961	S
Armenia	Soviet Union	1991	S
Azerbaijan	Soviet Union	1991	S
Belarus	Soviet Union	1991	S
Bulgaria	Soviet Union	1989	S

continued

New Nation	Old Nation	Year of Partition	Type of Partition
Czechoslovakia	Soviet Union	1989	S
East Germany	Soviet Union	1989	S
Estonia	Soviet Union	1991	S
Georgia	Soviet Union	1991	S
Hungary	Soviet Union	1989	S
Kazakhstan	Soviet Union	1991	S
Kyrgyzstan	Soviet Union	1991	S
Latvia	Soviet Union	1990	S
Lithuania	Soviet Union	1990	S
Moldova	Soviet Union	1991	S
Mongolia	Soviet Union	1989	S
North Korea	Soviet Union	1948	S
Poland	Soviet Union	1989	S
Romania	Soviet Union	1989	S
Tajikistan	Soviet Union	1991	S
Turkmenistan	Soviet Union	1991	S
Ukraine	Soviet Union	1991	S
Uzbekistan	Soviet Union	1991	S
Equatorial Guinea	Spain	1968	D
South Sudan	Sudan	2011	O

New Nation	Old Nation	Year of Partition	Type of Partition
Antigua/Barbuda	UK	1981	D
Bahamas	UK	1973	D
Bahrain	UK	1971	D
Barbados	UK	1966	D
Belize	UK	1981	D
Botswana	UK	1966	D
Brunei	UK	1984	D
Cyprus	UK	1960	D
Dominica	UK	1978	D
Egypt	UK	1956	D
Eswatini	UK	1968	D
Gambia	UK	1965	D
Ghana	UK	1957	D
Grenada	UK	1974	D
Guyana	UK	1966	D
India	UK	1947	D
Israel	UK	1948	D
Jamaica	UK	1962	D
Jordan	UK	1946	D
Kenya	UK	1963	D

continued

New Nation	Old Nation	Year of Partition	Type of Partition
Kiribati	UK	1979	D
Lesotho	UK	1966	D
Malawi	UK	1964	D
Malaysia	UK	1963	D
Maldives	UK	1965	D
Malta	UK	1964	D
Mauritius	UK	1968	D
Myanmar	UK	1948	D
Nauru	UK	1968	D
Nigeria	UK	1960	D
Pakistan	UK	1947	D
Saint Kitts and Nevis	UK	1983	D
Saint Vincent/ Grenadines	UK	1979	D
Seychelles	UK	1976	D
Sierra Leone	UK	1961	D
Solomon Islands	UK	1978	D
Sri Lanka	UK	1948	D
Tanzania	UK	1961	D
Tonga	UK	1970	D
Trinidad/Tobago	UK	1962	D

New Nation	Old Nation	Year of Partition	Type of Partition
Tuvalu	UK	1978	D
United Arab Emirates	UK	1971	D
Vanuatu	UK	1980	D
Yemen	UK	1967	D
Zambia	UK	1964	D
Zimbabwe	UK	1980	D
Somalia	UK/Italy	1960	D
Marshall Islands	USA	1986	D
Micronesia	USA	1986	D
Palau	USA	1994	D
Bosnia	Yugoslavia	1992	O
Croatia	Yugoslavia	1991	O
Kosovo	Yugoslavia	2008	O
Montenegro	Yugoslavia	2006	O
North Macedonia	Yugoslavia	1991	O
Serbia	Yugoslavia	2006	O
Slovenia	Yugoslavia	1991	O

REFERENCES

Adnal, Madhuri. 2019. "Countries That Have Vetoed the Most in the UN?" OneIndia.com. March 14, 2019. https://www.oneindia.com/infographics/countries-that-have-vetoed-the-most-in-the-un-2864642.html.

Ainscough, Michael. 2002. "Next Generation Bioweapons." *Counter-proliferation Paper No. 14*. Maxwell Air Force Base, AL: US Air Force Counterproliferation Center.

Aitken, Peter. 2022. "Taiwan Warns Chinese Aircraft Flying in Air Defense Zone of Russia-Ukraine Invasion." Fox News. February 24, 2022. https://www.foxnews.com/world/taiwan-chinese-aircraft-air-defense-zone.

Alesina, Alberto, and Enrico Spolaore. 2005. *The Size of Nations*. Cambridge, MA: MIT Press.

Alibek, Ken. 1999. *Biohazard*. 1999. New York: Dell.

Amadeo, Kimberly. 2022. "U.S. Federal Budget Breakdown." The Balance. Updated June 3, 2022. https://www.thebalance.com/u-s-federal-budget-breakdown-3305789.

Applebaum, Anne. 2020. *The Twilight of Democracy*. New York: Doubleday. Kindle edition.

Aslund, Anders. 2012. "Policy Brief: Why a Breakup of the Euro Must Be Avoided: Lessons from Previous Breakups." Peterson Institute for International Economics. August 2012. https://www.piie.com/publications/policy-briefs/ why-breakup-euro-area-must-be-avoided-lessons-previous-breakups

Baldwin, Richard. 2016. *The Great Convergence*. Cambridge, MA: Harvard University Press.

Berls, Robert E. Jr. 2021. "Civil Society in Russia: Its Role under an Authoritarian Regime, Part III: The Leader and Society: Prospects for Change." NTI. July 13, 2021. https://www.nti.org/analysis/articles/ civil-society-russia-its-role-under-authoritarian-regime-part-iii-leader- and-society-prospects-change.

Birstein, Vadim. 2001. *The Perversion of Knowledge*. Boulder, CO: Westview Press.

Buckley, F.H. 2020. *American Secession*. New York: Encounter Books.

Calhoun, Craig, Dilip Gaonkar, and Charles Taylor. 2022. *Degenerations of Democracy*. Cambridge, MA: Harvard University Press. Kindle edition.

California National Party. 2016. "Calexit Independence Movement Sees Exponential Post-Election Growth as Thousands Flock to California National Party." Press release. November 23, 2016. https:// californianational.party/calexit-independence-movement-sees- exponential-post-election-growth-as-thousands-flock-to-california- national-party.

Carnegie Endowment for International Peace. 2006. *The Biological Weapons Threat and Nonproliferation Options*. Washington, DC: Center for Strategic and International Studies.

Carson, James. 2018. "Why Did So Many People Die in World War Two?" HistoryHit. July 24, 2018. https://www.historyhit.com/why-did-so-many-people-die-in-world-war-two.

Charatan, Fred. 1999. "Biohazard." (Book review.) BMJ. October 16 1999. 319(7216): 1077. https://www.ncbi.nlm.nih.gov/pmc/articles/PMC1116867.

Cheng, Evelyn. 2022. "China Refused to Call Russian Attack on Ukraine an 'Invasion,' Deflects Blame to U.S." CNBC. February 24, 2022. https://www.cnbc.com/2022/02/24/china-refuses-to-call-attack-on-ukraine-an-invasion-blames-us.html.

Christian, David. 2011. *Maps of Time*. Berkeley: University of California Press.

Dalrymple, William. 2015. "The Great Divide." *The New Yorker*. June 29, 2015.https://www.newyorker.com/magazine/2015/06/29/the-great-divide-books-dalrymple.

Davis, Col. Jim A., and Barry Schneider, eds. 2002. *The Gathering Biological Warfare Storm*. USAF Counterproliferation Center. https://www.hsdl.org/?view&did=449520.

Dean, John. 2018. "Q&A with the Author: Prius or Pickup? How the Answers to Four Simple Questions Explain America's Great Divide." Verdict (blog on Justia.com). October 22, 2018. https://verdict.justia.com/2018/10/22/q-a-with-the-author-prius-or-pickup-how-the-answers-to-four-simple-questions-explain-americas-great-divide.

Denny, Elaine K., and Barbara F. Walter. 2014. "Ethnicity and Civil War." *Journal of Peace Research* 51, no. 2: 199–212.

Drew, Kevin. 2021. "Hong Kong Crackdown a Part of China's Larger Strategy." *U.S. News & World Report*. September 16, 2021. https://www.usnews.com/news/best-countries/articles/2021-09-16/hong-kong-crackdown-is-part-of-chinas-larger-global-strategy-experts-say.

Drexler, Madeline. 2002. *Secret Agents: The Menace of Emerging Infections*. Washington, DC: Joseph Henry Press.

Duffin, Erin. 2021. "Number of Full-Time Law Enforcement Officers in the United States from 2004 to 2020." Statista. September 29, 2021. https://www.statista.com/statistics/191694/number-of-law-enforcement-officers-in-the-us.

Dwortzan, Mark. 2016. "How Much of a Difference Will the Paris Agreement Make?" *MIT News*. April 22, 2016. https://news.mit.edu/2016/how-much-difference-will-paris-agreement-make-0422.

Fazal, Tanisha M., and Paul Poast. 2019. "War Is Not Over: What the Optimists Get Wrong About Conflict." *Foreign Affairs*, November/December. https://www.foreignaffairs.com/articles/2019-10-15/war-not-over.

Fisher, James. 1985. "NASA Fears Future Flights Could Drown in a Sea of Orbiting Junk." *Chicago Tribune*. June 9, 1985. https://www.chicagotribune.com/news/ct-xpm-1985-06-09-8502060298-story.html.

Florida, Richard. 2019. "The Geography of America's Mobile and 'Stuck,' Mapped." Bloomberg. March 5, 2019. https://www.bloomberg.com/news/articles/2019-03-05/mobile-vs-stuck-who-lives-in-their-u-s-birth-state.

Freedman, Lawrence. 2020. "How the World Health Organisation's Failure to Challenge China Over Coronavirus Cost Us." The New Statesman (UK Edition). April 5, 2020. https://www.newstatesman.com/world/asia/2020/04/how-world-health-organisation-s-failure-challenge-china-over-coronavirus-cost-us.

Frey, Carl Benedikt, and Michael A. Osborne. 2013. "The Future of Employment: How Susceptible Are Jobs to Computerisation?" Oxford Martin School, University of Oxford. September 17, 2013. https://www.oxfordmartin.ox.ac.uk/downloads/academic/The_Future_of_Employment.pdf?link=mktw.

Frey, William. 2018. *Diversity Explosion*. Washington, DC: Brookings Institution.

Fujimoto, S., T. Mizuno, T. Ohnishi, C. Shimizu, and T. Watanabe. 2015. "Geographic Dependency of Population Distribution." In: Takayasu, H., Ito, N., Noda, I., Takayasu, M. (eds). Proceedings of the International Conference on Social Modeling and Simulation, plus Econophysics Colloquium 2014. Springer Proceedings in Complexity. Springer, Cham. https://doi.org/10.1007/978-3-319-20591-5_14.

Garton Ash, Timothy. 2012. "The Crisis of Europe: How the Union Came Together and Why It's Falling Apart." *Foreign Affairs*. September/October 2012. https://www.foreignaffairs.com/articles/europe/2012-08-16/crisis-europe.

Gimpel, James, Nathan Lovin, Bryant Moy, and Andrew Reeves. 2020. "The Urban-Rural Gulf in American Political Behavior." *Political Behavior*. December 2020. https://www.researchgate.net/publication/338607779_The_Urban-Rural_Gulf_in_American_Political_Behavior/download.

Goldstein, Judith L., Douglas Rivers and Michael Tomz. 2007. "Institutions in International Relations: Understanding the Effects of the GATT and the WTO on World Trade." *International Organization*. 61, no. 1, (January 2007). 37–67. https://www.cambridge.org/core/journals/international-organization/article/institutions-in-international-relations-understanding-the-effects-of-the-gatt-and-the-wto-on-world-trade/A62FC1DB7553625D9A544C135AA34C52.

Gordon, Robert. 2017. *The Rise and Fall of American Growth*. Princeton, NJ: Princeton University Press.

Graham, David A. 2021. "It's Not Vaccine Hesitancy. It's COVID-19 Denialism." *The Atlantic*. April 27, 2021. https://www.theatlantic.com/ideas/archive/2021/04/its-not-vaccine-hesitancy-its-covid-denialism/618724.

Green, Peter S. 1992. "Federal Parliament Votes to Dissolve Czechoslovakia." UPI. November 25, 1992. https://www.upi.com/Archives/1992/11/25/ Federal-Parliament-votes-to-dissolve-Czechoslovakia/1607722667600.

Guriev, Sergei, and Daniel Treisman. 2022. *Spin Dictators*. Princeton, NJ: Princeton University Press. Kindle edition.

Harari, Yuval. 2015. *Sapiens*. New York: HarperCollins.

Harrison, Todd, Kaitlyn Johnson, and Thomas G. Roberts. 2019. *Space Threat Assessment 2019*. Washington, DC: Center for Strategic and International Studies.

Harsha, Dan. 2020. "Taking China's Pulse." The Harvard Gazette. July 9, 2020. https://news.harvard.edu/gazette/story/2020/07/ long-term-survey-reveals-chinese-government-satisfaction.

Helliwell, John F., Richard Layard, Jeffrey Sachs, and Jan-Emmanuel De Neve, eds. 2020. World Happiness Report 2020. New York: Sustainable Development Solutions Network. https://worldhappiness.report/ ed/2020/#read.

Herre, Bastian and Max Roser. 2013. "Democracy." *Our World in Data*. https://ourworldindata.org/democracy.

Hetherington, Marc, and Jonathan Weiler. 2018. *Prius or Pickups?* Boston: Houghton Mifflin.

History.com Editors. 2018. "United Nations." History.com. Updated August 21, 2018. https://www.history.com/topics/world-war-ii/united-nations.

Ingraham, Christopher. 2018. "There Are More Guns Than People in the United States According to a New Study of Global Firearm Ownership." The Washington Post. June 19, 2018. https:// www.washingtonpost.com/news/wonk/wp/2018/06/19/ there-are-more-guns-than-people-in-the-united-states-according-to-a- new-study-of-global-firearm-ownership.

International IDEA. 2021. "Democracy Faces Perfect Storm as World Becomes More Authoritarian." November 22, 2021. International IDEA. https://www.idea.int/news-media/news/democracy-faces-perfect-storm-world-becomes-more-authoritarian.

Jacobson, Louis. 2013. "Medicare and Social Security: What You Paid Compared with What You Get." Politifact.com, February 1, 2013. https://www.politifact.com/article/2013/feb/01/medicare-and-social-security-what-you-paid-what-yo.

Kafkadesk Prague Office. 2019. "The Czech Republic's Schizophrenic Relation with the Euro." Kafkadesk. March 18, 2019. https://kafkadesk.org/2019/03/18/the-czech-republics-schizophrenic-relation-with-the-euro.

Keegan, John. 1993. *The History of Warfare*. New York: Vintage Books.

Keeley, Lawrence. 1996. *War Before Civilization*. Oxford: Oxford University Press.

Kiely, Eugene. 2011. "Did Lugar 'Bail Out' NYC?" FactCheck.org. July 18, 2011. https://www.factcheck.org/2011/07/did-lugar-bail-out-nyc.

Klein, Ezra. 2020. *Why We're Polarized*. New York: Avid Readers Press.

Kopf, Dan. 2017. "If the US Unemployment Rate Included Everyone Who Says They Want a Job, It Would Be Nearly Double." Quartz, January 5, 2017. https://qz.com/877432/the-us-unemployment-rate-measure-is-deceptive-and-doesnt-need-to-be.

Kupferschmidt, Kai. 2017. "How Canadian Researchers Reconstituted Extinct Poxvirus for $100,000 Using Mail-Order DNA." *Science*. July 6, 2017. https://www.science.org/content/article/how-canadian-researchers-reconstituted-extinct-poxvirus-100000-using-mail-order-dna.

Lederer, Edith. 2020. "UN Failures on Coronavirus Underscore the Need for Reforms." https://apnews.com/article/virus-outbreak-antonio-guterres-archive-united-nations-united-nations-general-assembly-0848c3582913 62abfdce330b7b5e6420.

Lighthizer, Peter. 2020. "How to Make Trade Work for Workers." *Foreign Affairs* July/August.

Mahdawi, Arwa. 2017. "What Jobs Will Still Be Around in 20 Years?" *The Guardian*, June 26, 2017. https://www.theguardian.com/us-news/2017/jun/26/jobs-future-automation-robots-skills-creative-health.

Mahler, Armin, and Georg Mascolo. 2011. "Interview with Former German Finance Minister: 'Germans Will Have to Pay.'" Spiegel International. September 12, 2011. https://www.spiegel.de/international/europe/interview-with-former-german-finance-minister-germans-will-have-to-pay-a-785704.html.

Makamson, Collin. 2021. "The League Is Dead. Long Live the United Nations." The National World War II Museum. April 19, 2021. https://www.nationalww2museum.org/war/articles/league-of-nations.

Marotta, David John, and Megan Russell. 2019. "Protective Tariffs: Primary Cause of the Civil War." *The Daily Progress*. Updated May 15, 2019. https://dailyprogress.com/opinion/columns/protective-tariffs-primary-cause-of-the-civil-war/article_63b77f5c-dc0c-11e2-8e99-001a4bcf6878.html.

Martin, Jonathan, and Alexander Burns. 2022. *This Will Not Pass*. New York: Simon & Schuster. Kindle edition.

McKinsey Global Institute. 2017. *Jobs Lost, Jobs Gained: Workforce Transitions in a Time of Automation*. New York: McKinsey & Company. https://www.mckinsey.com/~/media/mckinsey/industries/public and social sector/our insights/what the future of work will mean for jobs skills and wages/mgi-jobs-lost-jobs-gained-executive-summary-december-6-2017.pdf.

Milanovic, Branko. 2016. *Global Inequality*. Cambridge, MA: Harvard University Press.

Mishel, Lawrence, Elise Gould, and Josh Bivens. 2015. "Wage Stagnation in Nine Charts." Economic Policy Institute. January 6, 2015. https://www.epi.org/publication/charting-wage-stagnation.

Molitz, James. 2019. *The Politics of Space Security*, 3rd ed. Palo Alto, CA: Stanford University Press.

Moon, Penderel. 1961. *Divide and Quit*. London: Chatto & Windus.

Moretti, Enrico. 2013. *The New Geography of Jobs*. New York: First Mariner Books.

Morton, Oliver. 2015. *The Planet Remade*. Princeton, NJ: Princeton University Press.

National Taxpayers Union Foundation. "Who Pays Income Taxes?" https://www.ntu.org/foundation/tax-page/who-pays-income-taxes.

Naim, Moises. 2022. *The Revenge of Power*. New York: St. Martin's Press. Kindle edition.

Office of the Surgeon General. 1997. *Textbook of Military Medicine: Warfare, Weaponry and the Casualty, Part 1*. Washington, DC: Department of Health and Human Services.

Oldstone, Michael. 2010. *Viruses, Plagues and History*. Oxford: Oxford University Press.

Osterholm, Michael T., and Mark Olshaker. 2017. *Deadliest Enemy*. Boston: Little, Brown and Company.

Otterman, Sharon. 2005. "Iraq: Oil for Food Scandal." Council on Foreign Relations. Updated October 28, 2005. https://www.cfr.org/backgrounder/iraq-oil-food-scandal.

Panetta, Grace, Olivia Reaney, and Talia Lakritz. 2020. "The 19th Amendment Passed 100 Years Ago Today. The Evolution of American Voting Rights in 244 Years Shows How Far We've Come—and How Far We Have to Go." Business Insider. August 18, 2020. https://www.businessinsider.com/when-women-got-the-right-to-vote-american-voting-rights-timeline-2018-10#1776-and-before-only-men-who-owned-property-who-were-mainly-white-christian-and-over-21-have-the-right-to-vote-1.

Pearson, Daniel. 2017. "Lincoln Was Wrong on Trade." *The Hill*. March 1, 2017. https://thehill.com/blogs/pundits-blog/economy-budget/321843-lincoln-was-wrong-on-trade.

Pew Research Center. 2018. "Eastern and Western Europeans Differ on Importance of Religion, Views of Minorities, and Key Social Issues." Pew Research Center. October 29, 2018. https://www.pewforum.org/2018/10/29/eastern-and-western-europeans-differ-on-importance-of-religion-views-of-minorities-and-key-social-issues.

Piketty, Thomas, Li Yang, and Gabriel Zucman. 2019. "Income Inequality Is Growing Fast in China and Making It Look More Like the US." The London School of Economics and Political Science. April 1, 2019. https://blogs.lse.ac.uk/businessreview/2019/04/01/income-inequality-is-growing-fast-in-china-and-making-it-look-more-like-the-us.

Pinker, Steven. 2019. *Enlightenment Now*. New York: Penguin Books.

Reuters Staff. 2020. "Fact Check: Clarifying the Comparison Between Popular Vote and Counties Won in the 2020 Election." Reuters. December 29, 2020. https://www.reuters.com/article/uk-factcheck-votes-counties-election/fact-check-clarifying-the-comparison-between-popular-vote-and-counties-won-in-the-2020-election-idUSKBN2931UY.

Rodrik, Dani. 1996. "Why Do More Open Economies Have Bigger Governments?" *NBER Working Paper 5537*. Cambridge, MA: National Bureau of Economic Research. https://www.nber.org/papers/w5537.pdf.

Rodrik, Dani. 2011. *The Globalization Paradox*. New York: Norton.

Rodrik, Dani. 2018. *Straight Talk on Trade*. Princeton, NJ: Princeton University Press.

Roser, Max, Joe Hasell, Bastian Herre, and Bobbie Macdonald. 2016. "War and Peace." Our World in Data. https://ourworldindata.org/war-and-peace.

Roser, Max, Esteban Ortiz-Ospina, Hannah Ritchie, and Edouard Mathieu. 2013. "Military Spending." Our World in Data. https://ourworldindata.org/military-spending.

Sablik, Tim. 2015. Economic Focus. First Quarter 2015. The Secession Question. Federal Reserve Bank of Richmond. https://www.richmondfed.org/-/media/RichmondFedOrg/publications/research/econ_focus/2015/q1/pdf/cover_story.pdf.

Salmon, Andrew. 2019. "In South Korea, a UN Command That Isn't." Asia Times. May 8, 2019. https://asiatimes.com/2019/05/in-south-korea-a-un-command-that-isnt.

Scharre, Paul. 2018. *Army of None*. New York: W.W. Norton & Co.

Scheidel, Walter. 2017. *The Great Leveler*. Princeton NJ: Princeton University Press.

Schumacher, Richard. 2012. *Free Trade and Absolute and Comparative Advantage*. Potsam, Germany: WeltTrends. https://books.google.com/books?id=U5nPkWSVpzQC&printsec=frontcover&hl=en&source=gbs_ge_summary_r&cad=0#v=onepage&q&f=false.

Scott, James. 2017. *Against the Grain*. New Haven, CT: Yale University Press.

Simmons, Katie, Bruce Stokes, and Jacob Poushter. 2015. "2. Russian Public Opinion: Putin Praised, West Panned." Pew Research Center. June 10, 2015. https://www.pewresearch.org/global/2015/06/10/2-russian-public-opinion-putin-praised-west-panned.

Smil, Vaclav. 2018. *Energy and Civilization: A History*. Cambridge, MA: MIT Press.

Spruyt, Hendrick. 2005. *Ending Empire*. Ithaca, NY: Cornell University Press.

Stanovich, Keith. 2021. *The Bias That Divides Us*. Cambridge, MA: MIT Press.

Stiglitz, Joseph. 2018. *Globalization and Its Discontents*. New York: W.W. Norton & Co.

Swaminathan, Nikhil. 2008. "Why Does the Brain Need So Much Power?" *Scientific American*, April 29, 2008. https://www.scientificamerican.com/article/why-does-the-brain-need-s.

Tasker, Peter. 2021. "Where to Live for a Better Change at Income Equality? Try Japan." JapanForward. November 9, 2021. https://japan-forward.com/where-to-live-for-a-better-chance-at-income-equality-try-japan.

Tegmark, Max. 2017. *Life 3.0*. New York: Vintage Books.

Tilly, Charles. 1990. *Coercion, Capital and European States*. Oxford: Blackwell.

Toje, Asle. 2019. "The Causes of Peace: What We Know Now." Nobel Symposium Proceedings. Olso: Nobel Foundation. https://www.amazon.com/Causes-Peace-What-Know-Now-ebook/dp/B07XKVR35Q/ref=sr_1_1?crid=16LUG8Z92KYZZ&keywords=the+causes+of+peace+toje&qid=1653847305&sprefix=the+causes+of+peace+toje%2Caps%2C90&sr=8-1.

Troy, Dave. 2016. "Is Population Density the Key to Understanding Voting Behavior?" Medium. August 22, 2016. https://davetroy.medium.com/is-population-density-the-key-to-understanding-voting-behavior-191acc302a2b.

Walsh, Bryan. 2019. *End Times*. New York: Hachette Books.

Wilkinson, Will. 2019. "The Density Divide: Urbanization, Polarization, and Populist Backlash." Niskanen Center. June 2019. https://www.niskanencenter.org/the-density-divide-urbanization-polarization-and-populist-backlash/.

Wimmer, Andreas. 2013. *Waves of War*. Cambridge: Cambridge University Press.

Wimmer, Andreas, Lars-Erik Cederman, and Brian Min. 2009. "Ethnic Politics and Armed Conflict: A Configuration Analysis of a New Global Data Set." *American Sociological Review* 74, no. 2: 316–337.

Wood, Tyler. 2021. "Moving Industry Statistics." MoveBuddha. October 30, 2021. https://www.movebuddha.com/blog/moving-industry-statistics.

World Atlas. 2013. "Countries by Number of Military Satellites." Worldatlas.com. https://www.worldatlas.com/articles/countries-by-number-of-military-satellites.html.

World Health Organization. 2016. "Smallpox Vaccines." https://www.who.int/csr/disease/smallpox/vaccines/en/.

Worldometer. 2022. "Countries in the World by Population 2022." Worldometer.info. https://www.worldometers.info/world-population/population-by-country.

Yardeni Research Inc. "Central Banks: Monthly Balance Sheets." Yardeni.com. https://www.yardeni.com/pub/peacockfedecbassets.pdf.

Zubay, Geoffrey. 2005. *Agents of Bioterrorism.* New York: Columbia University Press.

NOTES

INTRODUCTION

1. The foundational text about the size of nations is Alesina and Spolaore (2005) and is highly recommended, particularly for those interested in a quantitative analysis of the issues discussed in this book. While I disagree with some of the conclusions of Alesina and Spolaore (2005), the book you are reading now would not be possible without the research done by Alberto Alesina and Enrico Spolaore and reported in their groundbreaking book and academic articles. They sought to inspire others to explore further their theories concerning the size of nations. They succeeded.

CHAPTER 1

1. Merriam-Webster. "State (definition)." https://www.merriam-webster.com/dictionary/state?utm_campaign=sd&utm_medium=serp&utm_source=jsojso.

2. Worldometer (2022).

CHAPTER 2

1. For the background of the early history of the American Navy, see https://www.history.navy.mil/browse-by-topic/heritage/origins-of-the-navy/birth-of-the-us-navy.html.

2. During wartime, governments have historically borrowed massively, but those monies are just taxes deferred.

3. Scharre (2018), 38.

4. Keeley (1996), 54.

5. Smil (2018), 369.

6. Smil (2018), 369.

7. Smil (2018), 372.

8. Keegan (1993), 301.

9. Keegan (1993), 301.

10. Keegan (1993), 301.

11. Keegan (1993), 301.

12. Keegan (1993), 305.

13. Keegan (1993), 305.

14. Keegan (1993), 305.

15. Keegan (1993), 305.

16. Keegan (1993), 305.

17. Christian (2011), 458.

18. Christian (2011), 458.

19. Smil (2018), 365.

20. Pinker (2019), 451.

21. The "Long Peace" may not be as peaceful as it seems. For a longer discussion, see my book *Confused by the Odds: How Probability Misleads Us.*

22. Roser, Hasell, et al. (2016). See "20th century international battle deaths per 100,000."

23. Roser, Hasell, et al. (2016). See "National Defense Spending as a Percentage of GDP."

24. Roser, Ortiz-Ospina, et al. (2013).

CHAPTER 3

1. "North Korea GDP." Trading Economics. 2021 Data. https://trading-economics.com/north-korea/gdp-annual-growth-rate.

2. "Gross Domestic Product, 4th Quarter and Year 2020 (Advance Estimate)." January 28, 2021. Bureau of Economic Analysis. https://www.bea.gov/news/2021/gross-domestic-product-4th-quarter-and-year-2020-advance-estimate.

3. "How Many Cars Are There in the US?" Hedges & Company. https://hedgescompany.com/automotive-market-research-statistics/auto-mailing-lists-and-marketing.

4. Drexler (2002), 14.

5. Drexler (2002), 14.

6. Drexler (2002), 15.

7. Drexler (2002), 256.

8. Office of the Surgeon General (1997), 684.

9. Carnegie (2006), iii.

10. Drexler (2002), 242.

11. Drexler (2002), 237.

12. Drexler (2002), 241.

13. Kupferschmidt (2017).

14. Drexler (2002), 239.

15. Zubay (2005), 249.

16. "Smallpox Vaccines." World Health Organization. May 31, 2016.
    https://www.who.int/news-room/feature-stories/detail/
    smallpox-vaccines.

17. Oldstone (2010), 89.

18. Oldstone (2010), 89.

19. Graham (2021).

20. Osterholm and Olshaker (2017), 263.

21. Osterholm and Olshaker (2017), 305.

22. Drexler (2002), 242.

23. Osterholm (2017), 129.

24. Osterholm (2017), 253.

25. https://dewesoft.com/daq/every-satellite-orbiting-earth-and-
    who-owns-them.

26. World Atlas (2013).

27.   Harrison et al. (2019), 2.

28.   Molitz (2019), 54.

29.   Molitz (2019), 53.

30.   Fisher (1985).

31.   Molitz (2019), 53.

32.   Molitz (2019), 6.

33.   Molitz (2019), 54.

34.   Of course, this does not mean the cost of offensive weapons systems will necessarily decline.

CHAPTER 4

1.   Marotta and Russell (2019).

2.   https://worldtradelaw.typepad.com/files/lincolnmyth.pdf. This quote is probably apocryphal, but nevertheless reflects Lincoln's beliefs about free trade.

3.   Pearson (2017).

4.   Baldwin (2016), 74.

5.   Stigliz (2018), xx.

6.   Lighthizer (2020), 86.

7.   Moretti (2013), 6.

8.   Moretti (2013), 22.

9.   Milanovic (2016), 20.

10. Kopf (2017). The reported official US government unemployment rate most commonly referenced is U-3. However, a more accurate number is U-6, which includes "discouraged workers," defined as those who have looked for a job in the last twelve months but have given up searching, and those who feel they cannot find a job because of education or age; and "underemployed workers," defined as those who have settled for part-time work even though they want full-time work. The US government calculates (but rarely talks about) U-6, a number that is consistently significantly higher than U-3. Other nations follow a similar practice.

11. Lighthizer (2020), 90.

12. Lighthizer (2020), 84.

13. Lighthizer (2020), 84.

14. Rodrik (2018), 36.

15. Rodrik (2018), 36

16. Rodrik (2018), 136.

17. Rodrik (2018), 154.

18. Rodrik (2018), 107.

19. Schumacher (2012), 10.

20. Schumacher (2012), 10.

21. Schumacher (2012), 25.

CHAPTER 5

1. California National Party (2016).

2. California National Party (2016).

3.   Smil (2018), 307.

4.   Smil (2018), 307.

5.   Smil (2018), 307.

6.   Smil (2018), 307.

7.   Mishel et al. (2015).

8.   Mishel et al. (2015).

9.   Mishel et al. (2015).

10. Mishel et al. (2015).

11. The term *Great Leveler* comes from Scheidel (2017).

12. Some political leaders are focused on juicing stock market returns by cutting corporate taxes, which further exacerbates income inequality. In addition, it has been estimated that between a quarter and a half of all US corporate taxes are paid by foreigners, either indirectly as owners of publicly traded shares or directly by subsidiaries of foreign companies operating in the United States. Hence, the tax corporate cut did not "put America first," as a substantial portion of the monies went into the pockets of foreigners.

13. Gordon (2017), 39.

14. Taxes on wealthy individuals and businesses have been imposed on a temporary basis during times of crisis, such as the Civil War, but were eliminated once the crisis passed.

15. "Federal Receipts as Percent of Gross Domestic Product." Federal Reserve Bank of St. Louis. https://fred.stlouisfed.org/series/FYFRGDA188S.

16. Amadeo (2022).

17.   Jacobson (2013).

18.   Jacobson (2013).

19.   Redistribution of income may not technically be considered a public good. The use of public education, health care, or a transfer payment is rivalrous, as consumption by one person limits the consumption by another. However, even what is generally considered a public good, such as national defense, is to some extent rivalrous, as it does not protect all citizens equally. The residents of Alaska are not as safe from a Russian invasion as those of Iowa. Public education, health care, and transfer payments are public goods in the sense that taxpayers fund them regardless of use. Those who attend private schools and visit private doctors still pay taxes to fund public schools and health care. But transfer payments are considered by most a social and moral imperative to aid the less fortunate. This is why I consider redistribution of income, in its many forms, to be a public good.

20.   National Taxpayers Union Foundation.

21.   Harari (2015), 9.

22.   Swaminathan (2008). The average human body consumes about 100 watts, and most studies show that the brain takes about 20 percent of total energy available for itself. Most of that is used to fire the neurons that emit electrical impulses. However, a significant portion of the energy consumed is for what is known as "housekeeping," or maintaining the cells within the human brain.

23.   Some have predicted that machines will eventually become "superintelligent," or beyond all human understanding. The moment when a machine surpasses all human intelligence has been called "the Singularity," a term that refers to the unknowability of what is on the other side of a black hole in space. After the Singularity, proponents of this view foresee the potential for machines to take over the planet and get rid of us. An example sometimes given is of a machine designed to make paper clips. Once it concludes that humans are hindering its work by consuming valuable resources that otherwise could be used for more paper clips, the machine will exterminate *Homo sapiens*, Terminator-style. Rid of pesky humans, the Earth can become one big Office Depot selling a single product. I am skeptical of this view. In the end, regardless of how superintelligent a machine becomes, its smarts are a product of electrical switches; it is simply 0s and 1s. Humans are capable of adding and subtracting binary numbers and figuring out why a machine does what it does. Of course, doing so can be very time-consuming. Recalculating a hundred-layer-thick neural network a couple million times would take a squad of the best number crunchers years. But I do not believe that the most powerful machines of the future will be beyond all human understanding. We can always check the arithmetic—if we want to spend the time and money.

24. McKinsey (2017).

25. McKinsey (2017).

26. Frey and Osborne (2013).

27. Frey and Osborne (2013).

28. Mahdawi (2017).

29. Frey (2018), 340.

30. Frey (2018), xiii.

31. Frey (2018), 312.

32. New generations of workers may still have challenges finding employment. Part of the problem is that educational systems are failing to prepare the next generation of workers. For example, only 40 percent of high schools in the United States teach computer programming

languages. In my view, high schools should provide marketable skills for those not planning on attending college. In turn, colleges should provide marketable skills to those not planning on attending graduate school. Similarly, postgraduate degrees should focus on a profession, such as medicine, engineering, research, or academia. The days of all students with college degrees landing highly paid jobs just because they spent four years studying and taking tests are behind us.

33. The idea to use horses as an example comes from Tegmark (2017). I have expressed Tegmark's idea differently, but the basic concept is his.

34. Tegmark (2017), 126.

35. Frey (2018), 315.

36. Frey (2018), 317.

37. Frey (2018), 27.

CHAPTER 6

1. Otterman (2005).

2. Otterman (2005).

3. Quote by Benito Mussolini. Power Quotations. https://www.powerquotations.com/quote/the-league-is-very-well.

4. Makamson (2021).

5. "Troop and Police Contributors." United Nations Peacekeeping. By Mission and Personnel Type. Data as of March 31, 2022. https://peacekeeping.un.org/en/troop-and-police-contributors.

6. The Soviet Union boycotted the vote and the seat for China at that time was held by Taiwan, so the resolutions passed.

7. Salmon (2019).

8. https://www.nytimes.com/1990/12/02/world/mideast-tensions-us-won-support-use-mideast-forces-iraq-resolution-us-soviet.html.

9. History.com Editors (2018).

10. Freedman (2020).

11. "Treaty on the Non-Proliferation of Nuclear Weapons." NTI. Updated February 28, 2022. https://www.nti.org/learn/treaties-and-regimes/treaty-on-the-non-proliferation-of-nuclear-weapons.

12. Furthermore, NPT grants signatories the "inalienable right" to pursue a wide range of nuclear technologies for power generation. It can be difficult to distinguish where nuclear capabilities for power stop and weapons start.

13. Charatan (1999).

14. Ainscough (2002), 254; Davis and Schneider (2002).

15. Drexler (2002), 251.

16. Drexler (2002), 250.

17. Drexler (2002), 250; Alibek (1999), 8.

18. Alibek (1999), 8.

19. Walsh (2019), 208.

20. Birstein (2001).

21. Drexler (2002), 252.

22. Adnal (2019).

23. Adnal (2019).

24. Seventy-Third Session, 36th and 37th Meetings. 2018. United Nations. Meetings Coverage and Press Releases. November 20, 2018. https://www.un.org/press/en/2018/ga12091.doc.htm.

25. In Hindsight: The Security Council in 2019." Security Council Report. January 31, 2020. https://www.securitycouncilreport.org/monthly-forecast/2020-02/in-hindsight-the-security-council-in-2019.php.

26. Paralysis Constricts Security Council Action in 2018, as Divisions among Permanent Members Fuel Escalation of Global Tensions." United Nations. Meetings Coverage and Press Releases. January 10, 2019. https://www.un.org/press/en/2019/sc13661.doc.htm.

27. Lederer (2020).

28. A related, more complicated question is the impact of NATO on the optimal size of the Russian state. NATO is a purely defensive military alliance, so Russia should not have to spend more on the public good of national defense. However, if Russia wishes to make credible threats of aggressive actions against some NATO nations, then the existence of NATO increases the amount Russia needs to spend on the military.

29. Goldstein et al. (2007).

30. Morton (2015), 3.

31. Morton (2015), 3.

32. Morton (2015), 3.

33. Dwortzan (2016).

34. Walsh (2019), 138.

35. Garton Ash (2012).

36. Garton Ash (2012).

37. Garton Ash (2012).

38. Garton Ash (2012).

39. Garton Ash (2012).

40. Aslund (2012), 3.

41. Yardeni Research Inc., 4.

42. https://www.yardeni.com/pub/balsheetwk.pdf

CHAPTER 7

1. After the United Kingdom abruptly departed India, a British civil servant, Penderel Moon, wrote a book titled *Divide and Exit*. The thesis of his book is that the British were more interested in getting out of India than limiting the costs of partition. Moon argues that British civil servants believed that the partition of India and Pakistan was an intractable problem and feared the worst would happen on their watch. In addition, they thought separation was best negotiated between the interested parties. The mass migration and subsequent loss of life and property that followed in the separation of Pakistan from India has led many to question whether in retrospect the benefits of reducing the scale of India were worth the costs of achieving a greater consensus, particularly as India remains a country that in my view is too big.

2. Dalrymple (2015).

3. Green (1992).

4. Kafkadesk Prague Office (2019).

5. "Zanzibar." Britannica. https://www.britannica.com/place/Zanzibar-island-Tanzania.

6. Mahler and Mascolo (2011).

7.   Mahler and Mascolo (2011).

8.   Buckley (2020), 106; Alesina and Spolaore (2005), 81; https://www
     .omnicalculator.com/finance/gdp-per-capita#the-us-gdp-per-capita-
     vs-the-highest-gdp-per-capita-in-the-world; https://www.cairn.info
     /revue-de-l-ofce-2019-4-page-139.htm#. There is a divergence in
     economic growth rates between OECD (Organization for Economic
     Co-operation and Development) and non-OECD countries. This cor-
     relation holds for all OECD countries, large and small. It also holds
     for small non-OECD nations, about 90 percent of the total, but not
     for the largest non-OECD nations, which demonstrate no significant
     correlation between size and growth. It is true that the volatility of
     GDP is greater for smaller countries, due to a less diversified indus-
     trial base. Higher growth rates come partially at the cost of greater
     volatility in output year to year. However, over time smaller countries
     enjoy a greater degree of economic success in terms of absolute levels
     of income and growth rates.

9.   https://www.visionofhumanity.org/wp-content/uploads/2022/09/
     UNESCO-WEB-210922-1.pdf.

10. Buckley (2020), 92.

11. https://freedomhouse.org.

12. Buckley (2020), 69.

13. https://www.transparency.org/en/what-is-corruption.

14. "Corruption Perceptions Index." Transparency International. Accessed
     June 3, 2022. https://www.transparency.org/en/cpi/2021.

15. Buckley (2020), 139.

16. Helliwell et al. (2020).

17. Helliwell et al. (2020).

18. Helliwell et al. (2020).

CHAPTER 8

1. Spruyt (2005), 42.

2. Spruyt (2005), 46.

3. Spruyt (2005), 47.

4. Spruyt (2005), 47.

5. Spruyt (2005), 48.

6. "Stasi." https://www.britannica.com/topic/Stasi.

7. Spruyt (2005), 82.

8. Spruyt (2005), 82.

9. Spruyt (2005), 82.

10. Spruyt (2005), 82.

11. Spruyt (2005), 65.

12. Wimmer (2013), 280.

13. Pinker (2019), 305.

14. Pinker (2019), 305.

15. Wimmer (2013), 222.

16. Denny and Walter (2014), 201.

17. National Taxpayers Union Foundation.

18. Worldometer (2022).

19. "Island Countries 2022." World Population Review. https://worldpopulationreview.com/country-rankings/island-countries.

CHAPTER 9

1. "Statistics on Slavery." Weber State University. https://faculty. weber.edu/kmackay/statistics_on_slavery.htm.

2. "Statistics on Slavery." Weber State University.

3. Tilly (1990), 85.

4. Harari (2015), 101.

5. Scott (2017), 156.

6. Scott (2017), 261.

7. Scott (2017), 180.

8. Scott (2017), 179.

9. Scheidel (2017), 243.

10. Scheidel (2017), 247.

11. Frey (2018), 75.

12. Herre and Roser (2013).

13. Herre and Roser (2013).

14. Scott (2017), 156.

15. Scott (2017), 156.

16. Aristotle, *Politics*, Book 1. http://www.perseus.tufts.edu/hopper/ text?doc=Perseus:text:1999.01.0058:book=1.

17. Scott (2017), 157.

18. Scott (2017), 181.

19. Panetta et al. (2020).

20. Kennan (1993), 142.

21. Duffin (2021).

22. "Who We Are: Our Funding." Interpol. https://www.interpol.int/en/Who-we-are/Our-funding.

23. The US Federal Reserve Bank actually has twenty-four branches. The functions of these branches are somewhat of a mystery.

24. Kiely (2011).

25. "NATO Spending by Country, 2022." World Population Review. https://worldpopulationreview.com/country-rankings/nato-spending-by-country.

26. Naim (2022), 245.

27. Naim (2022), 246.

28. Guriev and Treisman (2022), 214.

CHAPTER 10

1. Fujimoto et al. (2015).

2. "Japan Oil." Worldometer. https://www.worldometers.info/oil/japan-oil.

3. Everett Griner. "Japan's Agriculture Imports-Exports." From: USDA Economic Research Service. https://www.merlofarminggroup.com/agri-view-japan%E2%80%99s-agriculture-imports-exports.

4. Tasker (2021).

5. Tasker (2021).

6. Tasker (2021).

7. "Population Estimates by Age, December 1, 2021 (Final Estimates), to March 1, 2022 (Provisional Estimates)." Statistics Bureau of Japan. https://www.stat.go.jp/english/data/jinsui/tsuki/index.html; "Basic Complete Tabulation on Population and Households of the 2020 Population Census of Japan Was Released." 2021. Statistics Bureau of Japan. December 28, 2021. https://www.stat.go.jp/english/info/news/20211228.html.

8. "Population Projections for Japan (2016–2065): Summary." National Institute of Population and Social Security Research. https://www.ipss.go.jp/pp-zenkoku/e/zenkoku_e2017/pp_zenkoku2017e_gaiyou.html.

9. Immigration Services Agency of Japan. https://www.isa.go.jp/en/index.html.

10. "Inspectors Knock: Getting a Passport Is Not Easy." *The Economist.* August 20, 2016. https://www.economist.com/asia/2016/08/20/inspectors-knock.

11. Pew Research Center (2018).

12. Pew Research Center (2018).

13. Simmons et al. (2015).

14. Simmons et al. (2015).

15. Simmons et al. (2015).

16. Berls (2021).

17. Berls (2021).

18. Gramlich, John. 2019. "For World Population Day, a Look at the Countries with the Biggest Projected Gains—and Losses—by 2100." Pew Research Center. July 10, 2019. https://www.pewresearch.org/fact-tank/2019/07/10/for-world-population-day-a-look-at-the-countries-with-the-biggest-projected-gains-and-losses-by-2100.

19. Piketty et al. (2019).

20. Piketty et al. (2019).

21. Piketty et al. (2019).

22. Piketty et al. (2019).

23. Drew (2021).

24. "China: Systematic Repression of Ethnic Minorities Laid Bare in UN Findings." Amnesty International. August 30, 2018. https://www.amnesty.org/en/latest/news/2018/08/china-systematic-repression-of-ethn.

25. https://reutersinstitute.politics.ox.ac.uk/digital-news-report/2021/dnr-executive-summary.

26. Aitken (2022).

27. Cheng (2022).

28. "People of China." From: "A Visual Sourcebook for Chinese Civilization." Prepared by Patricia Buckley Ebrey. https://depts.washington.edu/chinaciv/geo/people.htm.

29. Harsha (2020).

30. Harsha (2020).

31. Guriev and Treisman (2022), 192.

32. Guriev and Treisman (2022), 192.

33. Stanovich (2021), 140.

34. Stanovich (2021), 140.

35. Stanovich (2021), 140.

36. Klein (2020), 38.

37. Klein (2020), 38.

38. Gimpel et al. (2020), 14.

39. Troy (2016).

40. Wilkinson (2019).

41. Wilkinson (2019).

42. Reuters Staff (2020).

43. Dean (2018).

44. "Illinois Presidential Election Results 2020." NBC News. https://www.nbcnews.com/politics/2020-elections/illinois-president-results.

45. "Illinois Presidential Election Results 2020."

46. "Texas Presidential Election Results 2020." NBC News. https://www.nbcnews.com/politics/2020-elections/texas-president-results.

47. "Texas Presidential Election Results 2020."

48. "Texas Presidential Election Results 2020."

49. Wood (2021).

50. Florida (2019).

51. In fact, perhaps most would stay put, at least for several years. But that defeats the purpose of partition in the first place.

52. Ingraham (2018).

53. Ingraham (2018).

54. Naim (2022), 100.

EPILOGUE

1. Carson (2018).

2. International IDEA (2021).

3. International IDEA (2021).

INDEX

Note: References followed by "*n*" refer to endnotes.